Your HR Goldmine

How to Turn Your Human Resources Know-How Into A Lucrative Second Income & Make A Difference In People's Lives...Without Leaving Your HR Day Job!

Alan Collins

Success in HR Publishing
Chicago, Illinois USA

Copyright © 2012 by Alan Collins
Printed in the United States of America.

ISBN-10   0-615-54671-4
ISBN-13   978-0-615-54671-1

All rights reserved. No part of this book may be reproduced or transmitted in any form whatsoever including: electronic, or mechanical, including photocopying, recording, or by any informational storage or retrieval system without express written, dated and signed permission from the author.

DISCLAIMER AND LEGAL NOTICE: The information presented herein presents the view of the author as of the date of publication. Because of the rate with which conditions change, the author reserves the right to alter and update his opinion based on new information and business conditions in general. This book is for informational purposes only. Every effort has been made to accurately represent the contents here. Even though the information in this book has strong earnings potential, there's absolutely no guarantee that you will advance your career or earn any money whatsoever by using the methods and ideas in this book. Therefore, the examples in this book are not to be interpreted as a promise or guarantee of earnings or career potential. Such career and earnings potential is entirely depended on the person using the information in this book and the related ideas and techniques. We do not purport this as a "get rich quick scheme" or "get promoted quickly without doing any work scheme."

Dedicated to my son, Bryan.

Fifty percent of the proceeds of this book will go to the Bryan A. Collins Memorial Scholarship Program which provides scholarships to deserving, high potential minority students who excel in academics and in service to others. I encourage you to join me in supporting this truly worthwhile cause at www.BryanCollinsScholarship.org.

CONTENTS

	Introduction: How To Squeeze The Most Juice From This Book	1
1:	How I Stumbled Into The Exciting New World of Turning My Know-How Into Income	8
2:	The Fastest & Easiest Way To Cash In On Your Expertise in Human Resources	22
3:	How To Turn As Few As 20 Pages Of Your HR Know-How Into 9 Different Lucrative "Products"	33
4:	The First Step You Absolutely, Positively Must Not Screw Up	43
5:	Step Two: Pinpointing Hot Topics You Can Be Successful With -- Including 157 HR Topic Ideas That You Can Steal, Use Today & Profit From	52
6:	Step Three: Preparing P.A.G.E.S. Of Compelling Information That People Are Hungry For Now	75
7:	21 Ways You Can Compile & Create Awesome, Highly Desirable HR Information – While Doing Little Or None Of The Work Yourself	89
8:	Step Four: How To Package, Price And Position Your HR Know-How & Information For Mega-Success	99
9:	Step Five: Putting Together A Powerful Sales Message That Creates Huge Demand For Your HR Expertise, Advice & Know-How	115

10:	Step Six: How To P.U.T.U.P. a Website That Will Collect & Instantly Deposit Money From Your Clients…Without You Needing To Lift A Finger	135
11:	Step Seven: A Blueprint For Promoting & Building Your Second income Empire	146
12:	The Step-by-Step Plan For Getting Everything Launched In Just 7 Days	170
13:	How To Get This Done While Keeping Your Day Job in Human Resources	183
14:	One Final Word: G.O.Y.A.	193
	Connect To Us Online	195
	The Bryan A. Collins Scholarship Program	196
	About The Author	197

HR Career Success Resources
by Alan Collins

UNWRITTEN HR RULES:
21 Secrets for Attaining
Awesome Career Success
in Human Resources
*Download Two Free Chapters
Available now at:
www.UnwrittenHRRules.com*

BEST KEPT HR SECRETS:
400 Most Powerful Tips For Thriving At Work, Making Yourself Indispensable & Attaining Outrageous Success in Human Resources
*Download Free Excerpts
Available now at:
www.BestKeptHRSecrets.com*

START YOUR OWN AWESOME HR BLOG: The Absolute Beginner's Guide To Launching Your Own Human Resources Blog...Step-by-Step, Quickly & From Scratch
*Download One Free Chapter
Available now at:
www.AwesomeHRBlog.com*

INTRODUCTION

HOW TO SQUEEZE THE MOST JUICE FROM THIS BOOK!

The book focuses on five simple ideas:

1. The know-how, skills or experience that you've already acquired in HR is a *goldmine*…and one that you can turn into extra income.

2. The key to cashing in on your human resources talent, expertise and knowledge lies in being able to "package" it up <u>FAST</u>…and in a way that others can access it, benefit from it and pay you for it.

3. Once you've gotten paid the first time, you can repeat this process over and over again to literally build a second income empire.

4. You can do all this without ever needing to leave your HR day job by following the 7-day step-by-step plan laid out in this book. If you have a computer with internet access, and can find 2-3 hours a day across seven days, you've got everything you need to get started.

5. However, it's not all about money. You can create a powerful HR brand, a profoundly more meaningful career

for yourself and make a difference in other people's lives or their businesses by sharing what you already know.

That's it. That's what this book is about in a nutshell.

Obviously, there is a lot more to all this. But the formula is here. The method is here. The tactics, ideas, tips, techniques, inspiration and information are all laid out right here within the pages of this book.

There Are Lots of Legitimate Reasons For You To Maximize Your HR Experience And Know-How

First of all, it's tough to ignore what's happening globally as we speak. Massive unemployment. Skyrocketing gas prices. Home foreclosures. And people, in general, suffering like they never have before. Like me, you no doubt know many terrific HR people with world-class skills that have been pink slipped. You may know others who have had their 401(k) or retirement savings disappear overnight from so-called "experts" on Wall Street. Still others have had their dreams torn apart by a heartless economy. And it all adds up to fear and anxiety about the future for so many people in HR.

Years ago, you could rely on "the system" and expect that things would work out. But that sense of security has gone and will never return. The MOST important thing to realize is that you own the responsibility for creating your own job security.

That's where this book comes in. It's not the complete answer. But it can give a "starting point" in creating the kind of "career security" you need in today's economy.

What is fantastic about the approach described in this book is that it can work for you...*no matter where you are in your HR career right now.*

- You can be just getting started in your first HR job.
- You can be a 10-year HR veteran with years of diverse HR experience.
- You can be a knowledgeable HR specialist in compensation, labor relations, staffing or leadership development.

- You can be an HR leader, consultant, coach or part-time contract professional.
- Or you can even be a senior vice president of HR in a Fortune 100 company.

It just doesn't matter.

Really.

I'm convinced that just about anyone in HR can do this.

Ready to cut to the chase? Ready to dive into all this and get going? Ok. But before we do, let me highlight a few key points you should be aware of upfront.

A Dose Of Reality: This Is Absolutely NOT Some Kind Of "Magic" Get-Rich-Overnight Scheme.

I'd love to guarantee that you'd be able to read this book and the next day wake up buried in cash and job offers. I'm sure it would be simpler for me to tell you to just wave a magic wand, and say "abra-cadabra" – and "poof" – from thin air appears tons of extra income and hundreds of people beating down your door demanding to pay you millions for your HR experience or hire you at double your annual income.

It ain't gonna happen.

I don't own any kind of magic wand. Nor do I possess any magic powers. If that's what you're looking for, let me tell you straight up that this is nothing like that at all. There is no free lunch here. Yes, you can make a nice second income following the steps in this book. But this does require some work – typically a few hours on evenings and weekends to get started...and you can get this launched in as little as 7 days.

I know what you're thinking. The book talks about making a lucrative second income. What's that all about? Here's the deal. You CAN make an excellent side income at this and I certainly have. Unfortunately, I can't guarantee YOU any specific financial results. The FTC of our United States doesn't allow me to do this legally. And, my personal ethics will not allow me to do this morally. But the biggest reason I can't do this, by far, is that your second income depends entirely on your desire and how well you put the valuable information in this book into ACTION.

But with that said, let me say this.

It is possible for you to earn enough to pay your cable bill with this strategy? YES.

Is it possible for you to cover your mortgage payment with the strategy? YES.

Is it possible to earn a six-figure second income with this strategy? YES, and I'll even lay out a plan in this book for doing exactly that.

But again, let me emphasize, all this depends entirely on you. Everything in this book is a work of fact – but if, and only if, you do something with it. Otherwise, it's a work of fiction.

Just being honest.

Going Beyond Just Making Money: This Book Is Really About YOU Serving a Much, Much BIGGER and HIGHER Purpose in HR

In this book, I'm going to use words like *goldmine, making money, cashing in, profit, second income, multiple streams of revenue, etc.* I'll use these terms a lot. And, I will do this without one drop of shame or embarrassment. Frankly, that's why you bought this book.

However, this book is not ONLY about the money. It's about helping you create a profoundly more meaningful life – both for you and the clients with you will serve by sharing your knowledge and advice.

This book will enable you to get your HR talents and gifts out into the world, where they can be recognized and appreciated, beyond just what you're doing right now. It will allow you to help others attain success based on what you already know... and in the process make a difference in their careers, their businesses or their lives. And yes, getting paid for it.

You see, I don't think of HR as a job. Or even as a career. And it's certainly not as something that is owned by the company you happen to work for at the moment. I regard HR as a

calling. A calling because I deeply believe part of our life's purpose is to make a difference and lend a hand to those who are trying to live life productively and get ahead. Chances are someone extended a hand at various points to help you through your HR career. And if so, I believe you have an obligation to do the same and "pay it forward." What this means is:
- If you've struggled through setbacks in your job or career...and you've survived and learned from it, you should help those now struggling by sharing your lessons.
- If you've achieved the impossible, take some time and share the insights you've gained to make it possible for others to achieve the same.
- If you've spent years in HR figuring something out, why not shorten someone else's learning curve.
- If you have cracked to code to success in any area within HR field, why not let others in on your secrets?

All of this involves coming from a place of wanting to SERVE others by sharing your know-how to INSPIRE and INSTRUCT them in areas you've mastered or take for granted.

By adding value to people's lives and careers in this way you are helping them to get from point A to point B faster. Make no mistake about it, corporations, non-profits, executives and employees will always need help from knowledgeable HR professionals. If you fall in this camp, I believe your mission should be to create useful information, content and products that add value and teach them how to lead a better life or grow their business.

If you ever get confused about why you're doing anything in this book, come back and read this page.

I'll now climb down off my soapbox and move you on to my next point, which is…

This Is A Book You DO, Not Just A Book You Read.

While I'm confident you'll enjoy the stories, examples and insights laid out in this book… just reading it, or any other book, won't help you one bit. However, reading it and then taking action, will enhance your impact, income and career.

So, have your pen or a keyboard handy. Take a ton of notes while you read. You'll get lots of ideas as you go through the book that you'll want to act on later. Don't lose those because you got so excited that you had to plow on to the next page. You will want to underline, highlight or capture key points.

If you use 30% of the ideas in this book, you'll be ahead of the game. If you use 70% or more, you'll be golden.

Things Have Been Kept Super-Simple.
So Please, Don't Make Them More Complicated.

As you can probably tell already, you're not going to find much fancy writing in this book. There are no complex HR models with circles and arrows going everywhere. I'm a pretty basic, direct, down to earth guy.

I don't think it's helpful to distract people from what they're trying to learn with a bunch of fluff and $20 words. So what you're going to get is plain talk. Yeah, I know it sucks for entertainment. But it rocks for understanding. And, understanding and taking action is what this is all about.

If You Have An HR Day Job With A Medium-Large Sized Company, You Must Be Prepared To Deal With Two Critically Important Questions Before You Start.

These are:
  (1) Ensuring that you have carved a few hours a week in your spare time to work on this.
  (2) Making sure you are aware of the risks and ethical issues involved if you are currently working for a company that wants you focused only on their "company business."

I don't believe you should do anything that will jeopardize your job. So, I will tackle and provide answers and recommendations for both of these issues for you in Chapter 13.

Finally, There Are Some Shortcuts To Success.

To shorten the learning curve and speed up the pathway to your success, I've included throughout this book numerous templates, insider secrets, checklists and step-by-step action plans.

Be sure to check them all out.
Let's now get going.
Enjoy!

Alan Collins

Alan Collins

1
HOW I STUMBLED INTO THE EXCITING NEW WORLD OF TURNING MY KNOW-HOW INTO INCOME

Now that you know what this book is all about, let me tell you my story and four valuable lessons you can learn from it

It's a long story. I've never told it before publicly. So, I'd encourage you to read…

EVERY SINGLE WORD IN THIS CHAPTER!

I hate being so dramatic. But this chapter is that important. It sets the context for and helps you make sense out of everything else in the rest of this book.

With that in mind, let's get started.

This all began for me 15 years ago, while I was an HR manager at Quaker Oats. During the day, I supported our foods and our Gatorade businesses doing recruiting, training, and handling employee relations issues.

YOUR HR GOLDMINE

Away from work, I would relax and unwind with my hobby: collecting vintage comic books. They say everyone collects something...books, antiques, coins, artwork, purses, jewelry, high-heeled shoes and the like. And I was no exception. Since age 12, I'd been an avid collector of comics featuring Spider-Man, X-Men, Batman, and other characters which today capture headlines everywhere as subjects of top-grossing movies.

Having been at this for years, I had accumulated a sizeable collection. In fact, I had so many comics that they took up just about all the parking space in my garage...*plus* an outside storage space that I rented. And, even though I never had the time to count them, I would estimate that at my peak I'd accumulated well over 100,000 comics.

Yes, I was a real pack rat. My collecting addiction was that bad. And, it had totally, totally gotten out of control!

However, I didn't realize it until one day in February.

On this particular day, I had an important HR recruiting presentation to make to my boss (and his boss). And, I had misplaced both my presentation and handouts for the meeting. It had taken me two full days to pull this presentation together and so I couldn't easily re-create it.

Finally, after much searching, I found the lost documents buried in a pile of comic books in my bedroom an hour before the presentation was scheduled.

With presentation now in hand, I immediately rushed from home, neglecting to shower, and took the late morning Metra commuter train to work. Arriving at the office, I jumped in the elevator, and then barged into the meeting late. And, in my haste to get there, I looked a mess, and hadn't prepared well.

The result...

My HR Presentation Bombed! My Boss Was Pissed. And The Conversation I Had Afterwards With Him Was Not Too Pleasant. As I Left His Office, His Last Words Were: *"You Better Get Your Freakin' Act Together!"*

Except freakin' was NOT the word he used.

YOUR HR GOLDMINE

Obviously, this was a wake-up call. A wake-up call that I heard...loudly and clearly.

As much as liked collecting, I enjoyed getting paychecks and putting food on my table a lot more. So, I decided it was time to get rid of my comic collection. Not all of them, mind you. That would have been just TOO extreme. I wasn't prepared to go cold turkey. I was going to keep the cream of the crop, just a few thousand of my best, most collectible comics...and more importantly, a number that I could enjoy and easily store in a separate room in my home...*safely* out of the way.

However, this meant selling about 98% of my collection. This was going to be a chore. And, a lot easier said than done. Like most long time collectors of anything, I had developed a deep emotional attachment my collection. Candidly, lots of my comic collectibles weren't worth very much to anyone else but me, but because they were like "members of my family," there was absolutely no way I was going to trash them or simply give them away for chump change. But, I also knew that selling close to 100,000 comic books that were semi-worthless profitably wasn't going to happen overnight. Especially for someone like me, who didn't know how to sell them in the first place.

So, I was in a real bind.

At that time, there weren't many reference materials on how to sell comic books profitably. Yes, you could find generic information on selling antiques and collectibles, but nothing specific about selling comic books. I did all kinds of online research and picked the brains of all the experienced comic dealers I knew. I talked to those who were successful at selling comics. And, even those who weren't. Since no one seemed to have one clear answer, I just started doing lots of things to get these things sold. Anything I could think of. I got rid of quite a few on eBay (which wasn't nearly as popular then, as it is now). I sold some on consignment to other comic dealers. I put classified ads in newspapers. I set up tables on weekends and sold at local comic shows. I sold at local flea markets. I sold face-to-face. I sold them by mail-order. I did everything but go door-to-door. I fit all this in during my evenings and weekends, while continuing to do my HR day job.

Then, they did start selling. Very, very slowly at first. But it picked up. Anyway, in the process of selling off my collection, something else was happening that I didn't realize:

I was becoming an expert at selling comic books.

I didn't know it at the time but through trial and error, I was learning how to attract comic buyers and get good prices for my comics. This was a valuable skill that many experienced collectors and dealers were not able to do well. In fact, I developed a couple of methods that allowed me to quickly sell over 71,000 of my collection while making a pretty decent profit in the process.

However...

Around This Same Time, Something Else Happened That Helped Tie This All Together And Set The Stage For This Book And The Rest Of My HR Career.

I was attending a local SHRM meeting in a downtown Chicago hotel. Down the hall from the meeting was a seminar being put on by Robert Allen. You may have heard of him. He's the well-known author of the old best-selling book: *Multiple Streams of Income.* Allen has earned millions of dollars packaging and selling his advice and knowledge in real estate, investing and a variety of other fields.

The seminar he was leading that day was called *"Infopreneuring: Your Path To Creating Multiple Streams of Income."* Intrigued by the title, I left the SHRM session, walked down the hall, snuck into Allen's session and quietly took a seat in the back of the room to see what this was all about.

In the front of the room, on an elevated stage, Robert Allen described the *infopreneuing concept*. The word "infopreneur," he explained, combines two other words: "information" and "entrepreneur." And an infopreneur is someone who operates independently (like an entrepreneur) and takes the information in their head (e.g. their experiences, their skills, their know-how, their advice)...and turns it into income. They do this by creating "information products." An information product can be a book like this one. Or a special report. Or a workbook, instructor guide, audio CD, mp3, video, software, seminar, workshop or webinar. Or anything "packages" your knowledge in a way that allows it to be sold to others who want it. According to Allen...

The More Information Products That An Infopreneur Creates Based On Their Knowledge, The More Streams Of Income They Create Also.

His concluded his talk, with some great examples and by reinforcing the idea that your advice, wisdom, skills and expertise that you take for granted and use every day has tremendous untapped value -- but the key to getting paid for them is to turn them into information products so that people who need them can access them.

I loved his message and waited at the end of a long line of attendees to talk with him afterwards. When I finally got face to face with him, I told him I thought his presentation was excellent, but didn't know quite how to apply it. Patiently, he asked me a few questions about what I did for a living and what I did in my spare time. I told him about my HR career and my vintage comic collecting hobby. But, I added that I didn't feel all that knowledgeable. He told me something I've never forgotten and have repeated many times...

"Look, Alan, I have to hop a plane but here's my quick take on your situation. I think you believe you have to be guru or number one in your field to capitalize on what you know. You're wrong. **In the land of the blind, the one eyed man is king.** *You may not think your HR knowledge and experience is valuable, but it is to someone who has less experience than you do. Also, as far as your hobby is concerned, I'm sure there are lots of people who would be thrilled to know what you know about how to liquidate their comic book collections and make money at it. You could make a real difference in their lives. I really think you're sitting on a goldmine. If I were you I'd become an infopreneur in*

YOUR HR GOLDMINE

BOTH areas. I'd work on creating information products based on your experience in HR and on your experience selling your comic collection."

At that moment, a light bulb went on for the first time. I had never before thought about monetizing my knowledge.

And guess what I did immediately with this great advice I had received from one of the most remarkable experts I'd ever met? I did…

Nothing!

That's right. Absolutely nothing for six months.

Don't get me wrong. What he told me kept me up at night and bugged the crap out of me for weeks. But I didn't do anything with it...at least not right away. Instead, I kept selling my comics and consumed myself in my HR day job, so that was my excuse. Besides, infopreneuring sounded entirely too simple. Surely there had to be more to it.

Finally, I just couldn't get what he said out of my mind, so I decided to do more research about infopreneruing. I picked up his book and a few of his videos. And also books and tapes authored by Dan Kennedy, Jeff Paul and other gurus in the infopreneuring field. After soaking up their wisdom for months and after much soul-searching I finally made up my mind to give this thing a shot. I decided to stick my toe in the water.

I started small by typing up some short "reports" on making money in comics. These reports had titles like: *How To Make Big Money Selling Comics By Mail* and *Cashing In At Comic Shows*. Things I had done to sell my own comics. In all there were about five different titles I put together. I priced them from $15 to $29.95 each. In each one I shared my lessons, insights and tips I had picked up about selling comics. Each one was from 12 pages to no more than 40 typewritten pages. To my surprise, they were a lot easier to put together than I thought. And I was able to compile them in my spare time in the evenings or weekends.

YOUR HR GOLDMINE

I decided to sell these reports from a small classified ad in a comic book trade magazine called the *Comic Buyers Guide* that reached both comic dealers and collectors. This was in the early pre-internet days – before the proliferation of blogs, websites and online tools for selling merchandise that exists today. At this time, the best marketing and selling was done offline, not online. Since the magazine ad only cost me $42, I figured I had little to lose. And I hoped that as a comic collector myself, the reports I put together would appeal to at least a few comic sellers…

But Never In My Wildest Dreams Could I Have Imagined What Actually Happened.

A few days after the ad appeared in the magazine, I stopped by the post office to get my mail and…

I Looked Through The Little Glass Window On Door Of My Little Post Office Box, I Almost Dropped My Key!

The box was stuffed – jammed -- full of letters. Just about all of them containing checks, money orders, and yes even cash. I took out this thick wad of mail and saw that all the envelopes were all different sizes, colors and shapes. I was so anxious to get home and get a letter opener in my hands that I almost drove off the road.

Through this little project, I sold over 600 copies of my dirt-cheap reports and brought in over $12,000 in about five weeks. Some people ordered one report, most ordered two or three. At the time, a report I sold for $19.95 cost about $1.40 cents to print and $1 to mail. The $29.95 report I put together cost me about the same. *Little did I know that I had just discovered my goldmine.*

Now I have a confession to make. Today, over 15 years after I first started, I'm still selling this same information about comics. *However, we are now in the internet and mobile computing age.* I do everything completely online and on autopilot and it's more lucrative than ever.

YOUR HR GOLDMINE

Here's how it works today: People go to my website, read my sales message, click a button, and they order my reports. They can immediate access these reports in about 2 minutes directly from the website as soon their credit card is approved by PayPal. PayPal will then direct deposit their cash into my bank account. All of this works completely hands free…on auto-pilot…without me lifting a finger or doing anything. Orders come in 24/7, 365. I spend only about 2-3 hours a month just making sure things are still working properly.

Even More Importantly, In My View, Is The Tremendous Difference This Has Made In People's Lives.

I still get chills reading the personal e-mails from comic book collectors and dealers thanking me for providing such valuable, hard-to-find advice. In case you're interested (or just a bit curious) and want to check this all out, just go to my website: **ComicSellingSecrets.com.**

Three years ago, drawing upon the lessons learned from doing infopreneuring with my hobby…

I Decided To Become A "HR Infopreneur" Creating And Selling Information Products Based On My Know-How And Experience In Human Resources.

I knew that it would only be a matter of time before I would re-apply this model to HR. After all, HR was now my profession and one I was even more passionate about than my collecting endeavors. I'd been delivering Human Resources solutions in my day job for years and felt I had a lot of experiences that I could share.

So I decided that I'd start off my "HR infopreneruing" efforts a few hours a week in my spare time away from my HR job.

I didn't tell many people about it.

My first HR information product was a 20-page special report called the *"HR Recession Guide: 7 Ways To Recession-Proof Your HR Career & Avoid Losing Your Job."* I based this report on a hot need at the time. We were in the middle of the worst recession in 50 years and many HR professionals were losing their jobs left and right. Many of them were going to work in virtual fear of the ax falling. I thought my report would satisfy their hunger for career guidance during this horrible time.

In this report, I was brutally candid and pulled no punches in sharing my own experiences and tips as an HR executive, now at PepsiCo, for dodging the ax. It took me about eight hours to write up and finish it in one weekend. I created a website for it. The report itself wasn't very sophisticated and slick, but people appreciated the, no bull, "in-your-face," authentic advice I offered in it. Again, this was the first information product I ever put together drawing upon my HR know-how. I priced it at $19.95 each and was able to sell few hundred of this short report, with virtually no marketing…essentially just letting my LinkedIn network know about it and having my contacts spread the word. I now offer it as a free download to all my readers of this book as an example of a short report just about anyone in HR can put together. Feel free to use it as your own model. You can find it at HRRecessionGuide.com.

I then decided to take my HR infopreneuring efforts further. I decided that I needed a niche, something that would differentiate me from rest of the pack in HR. The success of my *HR Recession Guide* report told me that there was a hunger for candid, REAL career advice for HR folks, so I decided that this was the niche that I was going to serve.

I was not going to serve engineers.
I was not going to serve marketers..
I was not going to serve salespeople.
Just HR professionals.

This would become my "target market." This group touched a hot button for me as I was always thrilled and flattered to provide career counseling to members of my HR teams at Quaker Oats and PepsiCo and seeing them grow. So I expanded on the advice provided in my *HR Recession Guide* into a full-blown book called: *Unwritten HR Rules: 21 Secrets For Attaining Awesome Career Success in Human Resources*. I wrote this book in the evenings over a nine-month period of time. I decided to price it at $37.00 (paperback) and $21.97 (on Kindle). I was honored to learn that within one month of its release this book reached #15 on Amazon's list of best selling HR books. And, it has consistently ranked in the HR top 20 since that time.

I had now caught the HR infopreneurial bug.

My next step was to create a blog called SuccessInHR.com (after learning that my first choice, HRSuccess.com had already been taken). The purpose of the blog was to expand on the lessons contained in *Unwritten HR Rules* and to provide a marketing tool for it and another avenue to share my advice and serve my HR customers.

After I started the blog, my clients and customers started asking me how to set up their own HR blogs. If you've been with me so far, you know what I did next. Yep, you're right...

I Turned My Knowledge About HR Blogging Into Another HR Information Product.

I created a 20-page report on HR blogging that sold well. Later, I decided to expand it into a 60-page report (which I decided to call an e-book) and re-titled it: *Start Your Own Awesome HR Blog*. I focused it on teaching others step-by-step how to do what I did – even if they were absolute beginners. I sold 300 copies of this report at $37.00 in the first month it was released. And, it continues to sell consistently every month. It's still offered for sale at AwesomeHRBlog.com and took me a couple of weeks working evenings to complete.

I didn't stop there.

From there, I wrote *Best Kept HR Secrets: 400 Powerful Tips for Thriving at Work, Making Yourself Indispensable & Attaining Outrageous Success in Human Resources*. This book took six months to write and to publish and I priced it at $27.00. Like *Unwritten HR Rules*, this book has ranked highly on the Amazon's HR best-seller list as well.

I could go on. That's just the tip of the iceberg.

I've currently created 10 different HR information products that people pay me for and...

I'm having an absolute blast!

Now let me be very, very clear: I don't share any of this to brag. But rather to let you in on my story and why I feel strongly that if you're in HR you can do this too! You can turn your own knowledge into information products...working in your spare time or on weekends...no matter how much (or how little) experience you have. And this book lays a blueprint for doing this...in as little as 7 days.

Now that you know my story, let me now tell you...

**4 Valuable Lessons I Learned From
My Experience As An Infopreneur...And How
It Can Help YOU Cash In On Your <u>Own</u>
Experience in Human Resources!**

#1: People are absolutely hungry for "specialized information"...especially information that can help them solve painful problems. This is the biggest lesson I've learned about infopreneuring in HR. It has become clear to me that the human resources advice, wisdom, skills and expertise that you provide to your clients every day (and may be taking for granted) has tremendous untapped value. What you already know about HR *really is* your goldmine.

As you no doubt know, we live in an incredible information age where the demand for all types of information, advice and expertise has skyrocketed. In the HR space alone, human resources professionals, managers, executives, and consultants all over the planet are working on workforce, talent or people-related problems, issues and dilemmas. And because of this, the demand for HR-related information, answers, and solutions is absolutely overwhelming, exists like never before and is increasing every year. Everyday people are paying others who are more knowledgeable for solutions to their problems.

YOUR HR GOLDMINE

Just think about how much "expertise" YOU have purchased over the last year related to your job in HR. You've gone to seminars, workshops or attended a webinar or two. You've purchased books, reports and trade magazines. You've paid to download information online. You've probably listened to audio or video programs. You may have even paid for a coach or a consultant to bring in a different perspective or a piece of outside expertise that you didn't have. All of this is part of a growing industry...called the "infopreneuring industry"...populated by folks who are turning their expertise into income.

What this all means is that if you have just about any type of "specialized knowledge" or expertise in nearly anything related to HR, you're sitting on a hidden jackpot waiting for you to cash in on.

Frankly, this is the closest thing I've ever discovered to printing your own money -- legally! When I started asking for -- and getting money from what I already knew (away from work), I almost felt like I was stealing. Gradually, of course I've learned how important and priceless the right information can be and I have no problems at all charging what my knowledge is worth.

#2: You can become an HR infopreneur and provide information products in your own niche or specialty area. Though I've chosen "HR career development" as my primary niche or market, you don't have to do what I've done. There are literally hundreds of different HR-related markets and niches that you can focus on. And I'll lay out over 90 of them later on in this book.

#3: The number of ways to package, get paid for and make a difference with your HR experience is staggering. For example...

The first way you can get paid for your knowledge is through creating *written products*. That is people can benefit from your HR expertise through reading about it. This means you package your expertise into information products like:
- One-Page Tip Sheets

- Special Reports
- E-Books
- Books
- Workbooks
- Articles
- Newsletters
- Blog postings
- Instructor guides
- Transcripts.

The second way is through *audio products.* This allows your audience to *hear* your HR advice. You can accomplish this by creating:

- Audio programs
- CDs
- MP3s
- Conference call series
- One-on-one calls.

The third way is through *video products.* People may want to *watch you share your knowledge* on their television, computer, or mobile device. That means you might create:

- Webinars
- DVD home-study programs
- Online videos
- Webinars
- Mobile apps.

The fourth way is through *live or virtual events.* People might want to experience you and your HR message in person, which would lead you to create live events like:

- Seminars
- Workshops
- Retreats
- Adventures
- Expos.

Finally, there are *coaching products.* A segment of your audience will always want to master the solutions you are providing them and get a greater degree of access and training

from you. To serve them, you might create:
- Exclusive mastermind programs
- Coaching services
- Mentorship programs.

#4 -- However, the KEY to cashing in on your expertise in HR lies in being able to "package" it up <u>QUICKLY</u> and in a way those others can access it FAST... This is all about taking your current HR expertise and monetizing it, but doing it in a way that will not divert you from your HR day job or jeopardize it and can be done from your home in evenings or on weekends.

And, it is this last point – point #4 -- that I want to expand on in the next chapter.

2

THE FASTEST & EASIEST WAY TO CASH IN ON YOUR EXPERTISE IN HUMAN RESOURCES

You now know my story. You now know what HR infopreneuring is all about. You now know the variety of different ways to do it.

Let me now share the ONE single fastest and easiest way to profit from your HR expertise, which is the main focus of the rest of this book.

Here it is…

Find a HOT, burning, pressing problem that you can solve. And then, write up your "how-to" or "step-by-step" <u>solution</u> to that problem in a 20-40 page SPECIAL REPORT. Then sell this short report online in the $10-$40 range.

That's it. It's that simple.
PEOPLE PAY FOR SOLUTIONS…delivered FAST!

I've written books. I've created blogs. I've done HR consulting. I've given paid speeches. And, I know others that have created DVD-home study courses, audio programs, video programs, and successful coaching programs.

But the problem with all of these ways of packaging your talent is that they can be complicated, time consuming, and require a steep learning curve to get going.

Or require outsourcing to someone else to create for you.

Or require that you have a big reputation in HR.

Don't get me wrong, these are all lucrative ways to monetize your HR expertise. But simple and easy, they are NOT!

That's why short, 20-40 page special reports are your ticket if speed and simplicity is your goal. There is no easier and faster way to capitalize on your HR expertise than to convert it into a downloadable information product like a short, information-rich, special report.

Now wait. Before you dismiss this (like I did when I first heard it at Robert Allen's seminar), let me explain further…

What Is A Special Report?

First of all, it's not a book. A book is typically 120 or 300 pages and might take you months (even years) to write and publish. That's much, much too long.

Because a special report can be as short as 20 pages, it can be put together quickly.

Think of them as similar to the term papers you use to do in school. Remember when the professor gave you a term paper assignment. If you were like most of us, you waited until the last minute, pulled an all-nighter or two, but you finished it in a couple of days...and you still got a decent grade. Well that's exactly what a special report is. It's just like that term paper.

Special reports go by other names too. You'll hear them referred to as:
- E-books
- White papers
- Guides
- Manuals
- Instructor Guides
- How-to Guides
- Success guides

YOUR HR GOLDMINE

There is no ONE universally-accepted term...

**"WHITE PAPERS"used to be the popular term.
"E-BOOKS" is the hot term now.
For simplicity, I call all of these "SPECIAL REPORTS."
But, use whatever term you're most comfortable with.**

Just recognize that all of these different terms refer to the EXACT SAME THING: a 20-40 page written information product that provides the **SOLUTION to an urgent, compelling, or immediate problem the lives of your potential clients.**

Now, this ONE single solution you're providing can cover a step-by-step process, a technique or an approach that enables your client to:
- Go from point A to point B faster, easier or better
- Address an important HR pain point or dilemma
- Solve a difficult business problem or issue
- Achieve an important personal or job objective
- Save money or make money
- Attain career success or overcome career obstacles
- Gain enjoyment or satisfaction

Let me give you a few example human resources solutions that you could package into a problem-solving special report.

Example #1:
How To Use Social Media in Recruiting

Let's say for the last year you've been recruiting engineers and you used social media tools like Facebook, Twitter and LinkedIn to recruit them. You could easily monetize this HR expertise into a targeted, specific 20-page report called: "*How To Use Social Media To Recruit Tough-To-Find Engineering Talent.*" Hiring managers, recruiters, headhunters and HR professionals would be very interested in tapping into what you've learned if that can enhance their own success in recruiting. Imagine the impact you'd have on their ability to locate job candidates faster.

YOUR HR GOLDMINE

Special note: Chris Fernandi has done something very similar to this. Chris, an HR manager at EMC Corporation, took knowledge of recruiting and using social media tools like Facebook, Twitter, LinkedIn, Blogging, YouTube and Flickr and turned them into an e-book (again, just a special report using a different term) called: *Culture Convo: A Step-By-Step Guide To Employer Branding & Social Media.* He sells it for $19.00.

Example #2:
Twelve Strategies for Staying Union-Free in Your Business

One of biggest pain points that owners and operating managers in small to medium-sized businesses face is keeping their growing companies union-free. If you've had "union-free" experience and a successful track record dealing effectively with union organizing campaigns or creating work environments that make unions unnecessary…you are sitting on a jackpot. You could easily develop a 25-page report that specifically gives a step-by-step insider tips you've learned and used to help companies maintain their union-free status and create more positive work environments for their employees. You could even create different versions of that report to specifically address different unions. For example, one could be titled *"How To Successfully Maintain Union Free Status When The **Steelworkers** Are Knocking On Your Door"* or another could be titled, *"How To Successfully Maintain Union Free Status When Then **Teamsters** Have Organized Every Other Company in Your Area."* The highly specific and customized nature of these reports makes them valuable and powerful. You could easily sell these at $19.97 a crack…if not more.

Example #3:
14 Tips & Scripts for Facilitating Groups

Suppose you are a skilled group facilitator. You've had some success facilitating meetings with groups that want to develop their own business vision, mission and values. You could easily cash in on this your experience in this area – and help these businesses create more inspiring work environments for their people -- by putting together a 20 page *"Facilitator's Guide To Developing Vision Statements For Business Teams – Using Seven Simple Steps."* In this report, you could lay out your step-by-step process for facilitating these meetings including the materials needed, any pre-work assignments, how to handle tough meeting situations, etc. You could even create an entire line of short $20-$25 *"Facilitator Guides"* directed to business leaders that want to facilitate their own meetings, without a facilitator. These various reports would each deal with a different facilitation situation – e.g. running business ideation sessions, team building meetings, sales offsites or strategic planning retreats.

Obviously, these examples are just the tip of the iceberg. There are an unlimited number of topics you could choose to make an impact and an income from your know-how in HR with short special reports. And in the rest of this book I'm going to show you how to do exactly that.

But before I do that, I want to go much deeper and tell you...

Why Special Reports Are The Perfect Way To Create A Second Income and Cash In On Your HR Expertise.

Reason #1: They are super-easy to produce. As I've mentioned, a 20 page report can be done quickly. If you already have the knowledge of the topic you want to write about, organizing the information into a written format really only requires a few hours of your time...spread out over a few evenings or on the weekend. Even if you don't have all of the knowledge you need, doing the research to fill in the gaps is also very inexpensive, usually free and can be done almost completely online.

Reason #2: You only need to focus on solving ONE, single problem in each report. No need to solve all the world's problems. By tackling only ONE compelling micro-problem with your report, you can not only make it sell better, it allows you to create more short reports in the long run.

SIMPLE How-To Advice And Step-By-Step Answers To An IMMEDIATE Problem Are What People Are Demanding. If You Can Provide This QUICKLY and CONCISELY, You Can Make Some Serious Money From Your HR Know-How, Experience or Advice.

Highly-targeted special reports are ideal in today's short attention span world. People don't want to have to sit down with a 257-page book to learn how to solve a pressing problem. If you can help them solve their problem in 20 pages (or less), for an investment of 20 bucks, they're going to think you're a genius. Think about it like this: if you have a migraine headache, you want the solution delivered to you in the quickest possible fashion, you don't want to read a book, if you don't have to.

Reason #3: Special reports are simple to package and deliver. Here's all you need to do after you've created one:
- Simply turn it into a **PDF document.**
- Develop a **one-page sales message** that describes all the benefits it contains and that can influence and entice people to buy it.
- Put both the PDF document and the sales message on a **website** along with the **link to an order form**. (This website is where you offer it for sale and where people will pay you to download it.)
- When a person decides to buy your report, they click on your order form link, fill in their credit card details and this information goes to your **payment processor** (e.g. someone like a PayPal).
- Their credit card gets charged in a few seconds, and the customer is redirected to a web page where they can access your report and download to their computer.
- PayPal then automatically deposits their payment directly into your bank account.

Notice that you only need five things: a PDF document, one-page sales message, website, a link to an order form and a PayPal account and you're done.

This gives you a total "hands free" operation. You don't need employees. It operates on "auto-pilot," with no intervention on your part. Orders are taken automatically, your report is immediately downloaded once the payment is made and deposits are made into your bank account...all without any work on your part whatsoever. Later, I'll show you exactly how to quickly and easily get all this done.

Reason #4: Producing and delivering your special report costs you practically nothing. You don't have to break the bank or rob your 401k to get started. Unlike packaging your knowledge into a full-blown book, mp3 audio product, or a video product, or doing a webinar you don't need to invest any special equipment, technical support, or complicated software to get going.

Because your report is a PDF document, it has a couple of major cost advantages.
- First of all, you can convert your written report into a .pdf document for free. Again, I'll show you how to do this later in this book.
- With downloadable .pdf documents, there is no cost per unit. An extra copy of the .pdf document costs you nothing. If the customer pays you $19.95 for your short report, that whole $19.95 goes into your pocket (minus negligible credit card processing fees if you use PayPal or Clickbank).
- Shipping is easy also because you don't have to ship anything. Since your report is a digital document, your customer just downloads it immediately from their own computer immediately after buying it.

Reason #5: Your special report can produce income for you while you're working your HR day job or while you sleep. In your HR day job, you are rewarded for the results you deliver.

This is true no matter where you work in HR. If you work in a large corporation, a non-profit organization, or work for yourself as a consultant, the moment you stop delivering results, your job and income are at risk. However, this is NOT true with your special report. Once you've set it up for sale online, you can become lazy and practically forget about it.

The sales message does the selling. The order form takes orders, PayPal payment processing get you your money. And customers download the product to their computer…all without you lifting a finger.

And all this happens while you attend meetings with your boss, consult with your clients on HR issues or de-stress at home watching TV.

In this way, creating a report is a terrific way to multiply yourself, leverage what you know and expand your impact. You provide the solutions contained in your report over and over again to people who gladly pay you for getting them, instead of performing the service yourself each time.

Reason #6: Special reports provide instant gratification. We live in a want-it-now world. People are impatient. They crave urgency and speed. They are used to going into a store and walking out with what they bought as soon as they've paid for it.

Downloadable special reports align with this trend. And this is one of the reasons that they sell so well. The visitor reading your sales page knows that the product will be immediately received. They don't have to go shower, get in the car, and take a trip down to the bookstore to get the information. They don't even have to wait for Amazon.com to ship it to them after they ordered it online. No, they will get it *right now*. That's a big selling point for a lot of people. That's why the Kindle and other e-readers are so popular.

Everyone likes convenience and they'll pay extra for it.

Reason #7: Publishing your own line of special reports means you can call yourself an author and position yourself as an expert in your field. Experts are in high demand in

YOUR HR GOLDMINE

HR and being one allows you to expand your influence and impact. One person who has become an expert and thought-leader in her field...and one who has absolutely mastered this short report strategy is **Joan Stewart** (the "publicity hound")

Joan offers a collection of over 50 PR-related special reports. Most of them are just 5-10 pages long. She sells them for $10 each or $287 for the whole batch at **PublicityHound.com**. Even though she's in PR, not HR, her model can easily be re-applied by anyone in Human Resources.

Joan's story is a compelling one. Here's her story excerpted from an interview she did with Dan Janel, President and Founder of PR Leads:

> *When I joined the National Speakers Association, everybody said to: me "If you want to be viewed as an expert, you have to have a book," and I said, "I don't want to write a book...I don't have the time to write a book. I'm not interested."*
>
> *And they said, "Sorry, Joan, you're wrong; you've got to write a book." So she said, "All right, all right, I'll write the book already, but I'm going to start making money from the book long before it's published, and here's how I'm going to do it. I'm going to write a chapter, I'm going to call it a special report, and I'm going to post it for sale at my website for $7."*
>
> *So Chapter One is done. I'm going to write Chapter Two and I'm going to do the same thing. When I get 20 of them done, I'll go pedal the book, which is now written, to a publisher and see if it can get it published." Well guess what started to happen? I started my electronic newsletter at about the same time and these special reports were selling like hotcakes at $7 apiece.*
>
> *So, do the math. When I came to 20 special reports, selling for $7 apiece, how much was the whole deal worth? How many people do you know who can sell a book through a book store or any other place for $140? No one, including Tom Peters. So I hit on the magic for-*

mula. Not only did I throw the idea for the book out the window, I kept cranking out the special reports, and today I have over 50 of them, and I raised the price from $7 to $10 and I am flirting with the idea of raising the price yet again. I am not telling you don't write a book, because there are many good reasons to write a book. However, if you are writing your book strictly as a moneymaker, folks, you're writing your book for the wrong reason. Very few people make money from books. If you want write to make money, write special reports."

Let's summarize. In a nutshell, this is what Joan did...

She CHOSE a market, CREATED an entire line of short reports to serve that market...and then she CASHED IN and MADE A DIFFERENCE with her own know-how.

Keep Joan's model in mind. She has clearly demonstrated that the potential for scaling up your income selling short written reports is huge. And your chances for success are greatly enhanced if you have a vision for success.

Let me supply you with one. Here's a vision for what your special reports empire could look like 12 months from now:

1. You have 12 reports available for $10 each. (Simply develop one per month).
2. Customers buy the first one and, in time, buy most of the others. (Multiple customer purchases)
3. You put together package deals of 12 reports for $97. (Larger chunks of cash per transaction)
4. You get other people to help you sell your reports by launching an affiliate program for the $97 package (paying them 50% of what they sell) and sell large quantities of your bundle of reports. (Your affiliate partners will love getting close to $50 commission per order!)
5. You use your reports to launch "high ticket" offers that sell for $1,000 or more. (Skyrocket your profit!)

YOUR HR GOLDMINE

6. You make a "lucrative second income" with "short reports" (Yes, YOU!)
7. You build a following as a thought-leader in HR that makes a difference in people lives or helps businesses solve important issues.

Don't be concerned if some of this is confusing. In the upcoming sections of this book, we'll clarify everything and cover all of the steps you need to get this end result.

And what's great about all this is that...

Throughout <u>EVERY</u> stage of what we'll describe, you will <u>NEVER</u> be required to write anything more than 20-40 pages!

Once you've packaged up at least 20 pages of your HR know-how, you've truly created a valuable asset. To illustrate this, in the next chapter, I'll show you how you can turn these pages into a variety of lucrative products.

3

HOW TO TURN AS FEW AS 20 PAGES OF YOUR HR KNOW-HOW INTO 9 DIFFERENT LUCRATIVE "PRODUCTS"

Now that you know why creating your own special report is the ideal way to begin quickly cashing in on your HR know-how, we're going to take this a step further.

In this chapter, I'll show you how to take one short, 20-40 page report, change its format and profit from it in nine different ways. Here are the specific approaches that we'll cover:

1. "Niche-ing" your content
2. Bulking up your report into a book and selling it on Amazon
3. Converting your report into an e-book to sell via the Kindle and other e-readers
4. Chopping up your report into smaller articles & post them on a blog or sell them
5. Giving away your report for free and making it pay
6. Using it to grab free publicity
7. Turning your report's content into a live presentation

8. Turn your report's content in an entirely new format
9. Sell the resell rights to your report

Let's now break these down...

#1 – "Niche-ing" Your Content

Niche-ing is one of the most powerful and profitable ways to leverage the content in your special report. Niche-ing your content means that you tweak it to appeal to a particular niche. For example, if you've written a report on time management, you can capture a larger market share by tweaking the content to appeal to a specific niche. So your time management report could become:
- Time management for college students.
- Time management for business owners.
- Time management for new mothers.
- Time management for working parents.
- Time management for hospital administrators.
- Time management for CEOs.
- Time management for elementary education teachers.

And so on.

As you might expect, there are a nearly endless number of ways you can tweak this topic so that it appeals to different target audiences.

In just this example alone, you could take one report (time management) and create eight new products.

If you'd rather not do it yourself, then hire a ghostwriter to do it. Be sure to also change your marketing materials (such as your sales message) to appeal to your new target audience.

#2 – Bulking Up Your Report Into A Book And Selling It On Amazon

You can add more pages, illustrations, graphics and content to your report and guess what: you've got a book. If you have a

40-page report, you're at the half-way point to a finished, full-blown 80-page book...which is all you need. A solid 80+ page self-published book on a compelling topic will sell well on Amazon as a regular book or as an e-book on the Kindle or other e-reading platforms.

Imagine walking into a room and casually mentioning the fact that you just published your first book...and then whipping out your smart phone to show people your listing on Amazon.

Most folks have no idea how easy it is to get published on Amazon or on the Kindle, so they will think you walk on water.

And you'll feel like a rock star.

So how do you get your book on Amazon?

1. The process of course starts with 80+ page well-written book. No amount of publicity or promotion can make up for a poorly written and edited book. Compile your very best work and make sure it has been proofed numerous times by several people. Part of the stigma attached to self published titles is the poor quality of the copy editing. Don't be part of that problem. Take the time to edit your book thoroughly.
2. If you are publishing for Amazon the book will need to be in .PDF format.
3. The next step is to obtain an ISBN (International Standard Book Number). All published books are required to have this number. You can get one through Amazon for free or you can purchase your own for approximately $150. Having your own ISBN gives you greater flexibility.
4. Once you have your ISBN, you should design your cover and the interior pages. You can of course do the cover design yourself and Amazon has a built in cover design templates that you can use yourself at no cost. Or you can farm it out to a design firm for a more professional look. I use Accurance (accurance.com) as my book designer and they are tremendous! Book cover and interior page designing is a specific skill and firms exist which

specialize in this. It costs a few hundred dollars. While that seems like a great deal of money, it can be money well spent if you research well and chose the right designer.
5. So now you've got a camera-ready copy of the cover and the interior pages. The book is ready to print in the format Amazon requires. Now, it's time to visit Amazon.
6. Amazon has a site called CreateSpace.com. Set up a free account there. It is reasonably straight forward and involves answering a few questions. Once that's done all that is needed is to upload your book (both the cover and the interior pages) in the appropriate format and then register it. That's it. You now have a book published on Amazon!

#3 -- Converting Your Report Into An E-book To Sell Via The Kindle And Other E-Readers

If you're publishing on Amazon, you might as well publish on Kindle too. Why? Because Amazon announced sometime back that Kindle e-books outsell their paperbacks. So, jump on this trend by publishing on Kindle. Like book publishing on Amazon, publishing on Kindle is pretty easy.
1. First you will need an Amazon Direct Publishing account. If you are an Amazon.com customer, you can even use your same email and password. You will be required to enter your name, address, and tax information. You will also be asked the most important question which is how you want to be paid. Note: Kindle books come in a range of different sizes and accompanying price ranges. As long as you provide value and deliver on the promise you made in the title and the description, and as long as your e-book is priced appropriately, you can get away with surprisingly short books. For example, if you provide a simple solution to a burning problem and price the book at the 99 cents level, you won't have to

write more than a few pages or so. Just be sure that you do provide the solution you promised.
2. Write your (original) book in Microsoft Word. Word will allow you to save your file as an HTML file, which is the preferred format for the Kindle.
3. Make sure you edit your book for misspellings, grammar and typos. Pass it on to friends who will look through it for errors. If you can afford it, hire a proofreader. Amazon doesn't edit reports so if you make mistakes, they pass right on to your readers.
4. If you don't already have a user's account on Amazon, set one up. Once you have an account, you can publish to their digital platform. Go to dtp.amazon.com and sign in. Download their DTP Quickstart Guide. Follow the instructions for uploading your Word document. Alternatively, you can upload a PDF, a text file, or an HTML file. PDF files may not display well on the Kindle, so I recommend you go with HTML or a Word document. Since most people don't write in HTML, Word is the popular option.
5. Amazon lets you add your book title, description, price, and author bio when uploading your manuscript. Here's your chance to get your marketing message out there. What you enter here will show up on your book's Amazon page, so give it some long thought before submitting. If you don't have all the information now, you can save it at any point and come back to it later to complete the publication process.
6. Through your account on Amazon's digital platform, you can monitor sales and royalties. Pricing your report for maximum sales on Kindle may seem confusing at first. If you have a lot of competition in your topic, maybe cheap is better, like .99 to 2.99. If your subject is more esoteric, but in demand, you can ask more. You can always go back and change your price down the road. I recommend testing your initial price for a month and measuring sales.

Test a new price the next month and measure sales again. If price didn't seem to matter, go with the higher price.
7. Once your book is live on Amazon, consider putting up a Facebook page using the same keywords as in your title. Do the same with a Twitter account. Create a community around your topic so that people will see you as a resource and want to follow you.
8. All that is left to do is for you to promote your e-book. This can be as simple as telling your family and friends or it can be as complicated as a ten page marketing plan. The point is that success of your e-book depends not only on the quality of the work, but also that amount of work you put into getting the word out. That's it. You now have an e-book published on Kindle. And you thought the hard part was writing it!

#4 -- Chop Up Your Report Into Smaller Articles & Post Them On A Blog Or Sell Them

Let's now go in the opposite direction from publishing a book or an e-book.

For example, suppose you've created a 20-page report on improving employee retention and it contains 20 tips – with each tip about one page. You can chop up this report into 20 smaller articles and upload them to a blog and these can become 20 different blog posts. With these 20 posts, you've created an awesome blog…and enough information that people will come back often to see if you've posted something new. Your own blog is a valuable asset that can position you as an expert…and serves as a great marketing tool that can broaden your network and attract job, consulting and speaking opportunities.

Here's another way to use those 20 articles. Sign up for a service like Constánt Content (constantcontent.com) and sell them there. By giving them "usage rights," you can make $7 to $20 per article (before Constant Content's cut). They make their money by charging others to USE your content, but you still own it and can use it wherever else you want. You can make some real money on your articles. If you have 20 articles they accept, you could make as much as $400...and still use all the other methods in this book! According to them, 70% of their articles sell. But, they are VERY PICKY, so don't submit junk.

#5 – Give Away Your Report For Free & Make It Pay

In *101 Weird Ways To Make Money*, the author Steve Gillman describes an unusual way to profit from your report. A method you can easily re-apply with any HR-related report.

Steve shares that he once spent two days writing a 40-page report on Meditation. It had 30 short chapters. Here's what happened next:

(1) He put each one of those 30 chapters on a separate web page that readers could only access with a link he provided.
(2) Then he "monetized" those 30 pages by adding google pay-per-click ads to them.
(3) He then prepared 30 separate e-mails – each one containing a short sales message and a link to a different chapter. He then loaded these e-mails into an auto-responder.
(4) The auto-responder would then send out e-mail messages automatically, one per week in this case.
(5) He then put together a sales page, offering a "free subscription" to 30 chapters on Meditation. And by signing up, subscribers would get an e-mail each week with a link to a different chapter...along with an option to buy his complete report for $20 if they liked.

As he predicted, subscribers liked what they read so much, they couldn't wait 30 weeks for each chapter to arrive...they wanted it all right away! And, many bought his complete $20 report.

The Lesson: Steve made money two ways from this one report. By simply providing a free version, broken up into tiny chapters, he made money from buyers who clicked on the google pay-per-click ads...and he also profited from people who were impatient and decided to order the $20 paid report. Brilliant!

YOUR HR GOLDMINE

#6 -- Use It To Grab Some Free Publicity

Use pieces of your report content as a way to get yourself some free publicity. Here are two ideas you can use:
- You could use your content as the basis for a press release. Then you can submit this newsworthy item to your local news media as well as on distribution sites like PRWeb.com.
- Another way to use this content is to create professional, polished articles. Then submit these articles to popular offline niche magazines and newspapers.

Getting published in these publications means you get paid. But even more important, you get free publicity. You can establish yourself as an expert by getting frequently published in offline magazines. And yeah, it also impresses the heck out of people at parties.

#7 -- Turn Your Content Into A Live Presentation

You can easily turn your report's content into a live presentation. Then you can give this live presentation via a teleseminar, webinar or even as a speaking engagement (either free or for pay).

You might be a guest speaker at your local SHRM chapter, or you might create a free workshop or lunch-and-learn program.

Whatever you choose, the idea is to give useful and value added information. Your goal is to build a list of prospects, by making people "register" for your free presentation.

Then at the end of your talk, you can encourage people to buy your reports and/or join your paid workshop. And since you have everyone's contact information, you can also follow up and upsell them on other products that you will create later.

#8 -- Turn Your Content
Into An Entirely New Format

If you've given a live presentation based on your report, by making sure it's recorded you can then them it into a completely new

product that you can sell over and over. For example, you could:
- Turn your live presentation, seminar or webinar into a downloadable MP3.
- Create physical CDs from your audio recordings.
- Turn it into a video product by matching the audio and then adding some graphics, charts, slides, etc. This then could become a downloadable and streaming video or physical DVDs that you ship.

The reasons for doing this are simple:

1. **Changing the medium also means you can meet the needs of those with different learning styles and preferences.** For example, some people have a hard time remembering what they've read, but they love watching videos... and some people are just the opposite.
2. **Changing the format often means you change the perceived value of the product, which means you can charge more.** Generally, audio has a higher perceived value than text-only content, and videos are judged to be more valuable than text. So if you turn a text report into a video, you can usually charge much more for it.

Of course you can have the best of both words, simply by creating a hybrid product. You offer a product that's part digital and part written. It reduces refunds and boosts the perceived value. That's a win-win situation for you and your customers!

#9 -- Sell The Resell or Private Label Rights To Your Content

The ninth way to leverage the content in your report is instead of selling it to end users (i.e., your target audience), you sell the "rights" to your content to other marketers.

There are a couple of different types of rights you can offer:

Resell Rights: You can give other marketers the rights to SELL YOUR REPORT DIRECTLY TO THEIR CUSTOMERS, but they cannot change your content in any way. *Example:* You sell the "resell rights" to a $20 report that you've authored for a designated price, say $150. And, each purchaser can sell it in any fashion they see fit, for any price they choose and keep all the money as long as they don't alter the content. In this example, selling resell rights to 20 people can earn you a quick $3000.

Private Label Rights: This is different than resell rights in that not only do you give other people the right to resell or even giveaway your content, they also have the right to MODIFY OR CHANGE THE CONTENT in any way they see fit, including the right to put their name on the report as its AUTHOR. Private label rights are generally more desirable by purchasers. Because of this, you can generally earn 20-30 times the price of your report by selling the private label rights to it. This means for a 30 page report priced at $20, you could sell the private label rights at $400-600 a crack. And, you can sell these rights to as many people as you'd like as long as you let each buyer know how many total "rights" packages are being sold. This is only fair because the "uniqueness" and "value" of your content becomes diluted as more people purchase private label rights to it.

Selling rights to written content is a big, big business. By googling, "resale rights," "PLR" or "private label rights" you'll learn a great deal about the popularity of this approach. If you had an emergency come up and you just needed to raise some quick cash, then you might consider selling the rights to your existing reports. You'll find plenty of customers.

There you have it: 9 different, powerful and profitable ways to leverage the content in your special report. There's a lot here to chew on. So, in the next chapter, let's begin simplifying things by covering the step-by-step process for getting you started.

4

THE FIRST STEP YOU ABSOUTELY, POSTIVELY MUST NOT SCREW UP

Hopefully, you're sold on the power and potential of special reports. We're now going to provide you with a step-by-step roadmap for successfully planning, packaging, promoting and getting paid for the reports you will create. And here it is:

Step #1: Pick Your Target Audience
Step #2: Pinpoint Your Topic
Step #3: Prepare P.A.G.E.S. of High-Quality Information
Step #4: Package, Price and Position Your Information
Step #5: Put Together Your Sales Message
Step #6: P.U.T.-U.P. A Web Site So You Can Get Paid
Step #7: Promote & Build Your Second Income Empire

In the chapters that follow, we will get tactical and discuss every single one of these 7 steps in detail…starting with…

STEP 1: PICK YOUR TARGET AUDIENCE

Let's clarify some terms.

An "audience" is a group of people (or customers) that you will serve with your special reports such as:
- Business leaders
- Recruiters
- Engineers.

A "market" is simply a broad topic like:
- Team building
- Hiring & Recruitment
- Career advancement

However, a "target audience" combines both "audience" and "market." It's an *audience* interested in a particular *market*. Examples:
- Leaders interested in building better teams
- Recruiters interested in hiring talented employees
- Engineers wanting to advance their careers

You don't want to mess this step up. What you want to do is determine what target audience is best for you FIRST before you begin to write even one word of your report because.....

**Longer Term, You Will Want To Create
<u>Multiple</u>, <u>Related</u> Special Reports That Will Serve Them!**

For example, if your target audience consists of "recruiters interested in hiring talented employees," you can start with one and then create an entire line of short reports covering such topics as:

- Effective campus recruiting
- Using social media in recruiting
- Recruiting passive job candidates
- Using psychological tests in recruiting
- How to save money when using third party recruiters

...or any number of other recruiting topics directed at that target audience. Most people who write FIRST and find their target audience later, are surprised when they discover that they've written for an audience that's just not interested. Don't fall into this common trap.

3 Simple Rules for Choosing A Target Audience

I have three simple criteria that I look for in deciding what target audience I want to focus on.

1. A target audience accustomed to spending money. If the audience isn't accustomed to spending money – and, generally, a lot of money, then there's no point in directing any effort towards them. *"College students"* isn't a great target audience simply because most of them are broke! On the other hand, *"Engineers," "Accountants," "Small business owners,"* or other *"HR professionals"* spend a gazillion dollars each year on their own professional or business development…so they are a much more lucrative audience to go after.

2. A target audience that can be offered a wide variety of offers. If the audience limited in what you can sell to it, then again there is a red flag. You want to be able to present multiple offers related to the general theme of the target audience you have selected.

3. A target audience that you are passionate about. Frankly, some people would tell you that this isn't absolutely necessary. And they're right. If you can find a target audience or market that meets points 1 and 2, you're golden. However, I personally believe in putting your heart into everything you do. And if you can, that's a huge plus and that will just cement your decision. For example:

- If you find yourself frequently reading leadership books, then that's a hint that leadership may be a market you may want to concentrate on.

- If you're a work-at-home HR professional and you're always networking and sharing tips with others who also work at home, there's another hint.
- If you own lots of audio books and mp3s on teamwork and team building, why not focus on this topic and go help others learn what you have learned?
- If you're passionate about speaking or giving presentations, workshops or seminars, then you are already "doing" your topic. If you're good on your feet and get positive feedback on your speaking performances, why not share your insights with others who are scared to death when asked to speak in public.
- Have you had a turning point, a triumph, an "aha moment" or a tragedy in your career that makes you say: "Wow, this was a painful situation, but I handled it successfully." If so, then why not teach others so that they can overcome similar struggles?
- Ponder this: If you were to die at the end of this year, what message would you want to communicate to the world? What advice would you give others about their personal and professional lives? What message do you believe everyone in your target audience, perhaps the world, needs to hear? Why not share it.

Choosing a target audience is like choosing a calling in life -- sometimes it chooses you more than you choose it. That's why I want to give you some markets and audiences to consider in deciding upon the focus of your special reports. Here you go...

**A Starter List of 90+ Hot, Profitable Audiences
& Markets For Human Resources Professionals**
(Listed alphabetically)

AUDIENCES (*specific groups of people you can serve*)
- Administrative Assistants
- Asians in the Workplace
- Blacks in the Workplace

YOUR HR GOLDMINE

- Business Leaders (in Marketing, Sales, or R&D, etc.)
- CEOs
- Compensation & Benefit Professionals
- Consultants
- Entrepreneurs
- Executive Coaches
- Headhunters
- Hiring Managers
- HR Consultants
- HR Executives
- HR Managers
- HR Professionals
- Labor Relations Professionals
- Latinos in the Workplace
- LGBT Employees
- New Managers
- Organization Development Professionals
- Recruiters
- Retirees / Those Retirement-Bound
- Part-Time or Temporary Employees
- People in Transition / Job Seekers
- Professionals (in Marketing, Sales, IT or R&D, etc.)
- Social Media Newbies
- Telecommuters / Work-From-Home Professionals
- Women in the Workplace

MARKETS (*HR topics of potential interest to audiences*)
- Adult Learning & Training
- Absenteeism / Attendance Improvement
- Accident Reduction & Safety
- Being Organized
- Branding Yourself
- Building Relationships
- Building Teams / Teamwork
- Career Advancement
- Coaching
- Compensating Employees

YOUR HR GOLDMINE

- Communicating Persuasively
- Consulting
- Corporate Restructuring
- Cutting Costs
- Disabilities at Work
- Diversity & Inclusion
- Downsizing & Layoffs
- Employee Benefit Programs
- Employee Engagement
- Employee Surveys
- Employer Branding
- Executive Coaching
- Ethics, Values & Standards
- Expatriates
- Gen Xs in the Workplace
- Gen Ys in the Workplace
- Getting Promoted
- Goal & Objective-Setting
- Health Care for Employees
- High Performance Systems
- HR Certification
- HR Consultants
- HR Strategy
- HR Info Systems (HRIS)
- Improving Productivity
- Interviewing
- Job Search / Finding A Job
- Labor Relations / Unions
- Leading / Being A Leader
- Learning & Development
- Managing Change
- Mentoring
- Mergers & Acquisitions
- Onboarding New Employees
- Organization Development
- Performance Appraisals
- Persuasion & Influence

YOUR HR GOLDMINE

- Positive Employee Relations
- Professional Development
- Project Management
- Recruiting Strategies
- Retaining Talent / Turnover
- Selling Your Ideas
- Sexual Harassment
- Social Media in HR
- Strategic Planning
- Succession Planning
- Talent Management
- Time Management
- Total Reward Strategies
- Training (online approaches)
- Training (offline approaches)
- Union-Free / Avoidance
- Work/Life Balance
- Workplace Violence

Again, this is just a starter list. There are literally hundreds of other audiences and markets you can go after.

Depending on your HR experience, you can choose to create B2B (business-to-business) reports aimed at specific audiences such as non-profit associations, small businesses, entrepreneurs or consultants. Or you can create consumer reports geared at individuals such as engineers, salespeople, plant managers or other HR types. Or you can offer both.

In the B2B arena, for example, there are tons of small to medium-sized businesses that could no doubt benefit from guidance on HR issues. Many can't afford a full-time HR professional or a high-priced consultant. Nevertheless, they could certainly profit from your knowledge about C.O.B.R.A. compliance, or dealing with inappropriate employee behavior, or how to avoid wrongful termination suits, or how to create employment contracts. The sky's the limit. I'm sure you could come up with many more potential topics for your reports.

YOUR HR GOLDMINE

On the plus side, the B2B reports will likely fetch a much higher price than consumer reports. You can target these reports to specific business types with very little extra work.

Specific issue + Specific business type = Premium price.

Small businesses are always looking for ways to make their lives simpler and avoid red tape -- without paying high-priced consultants. What's more, they won't worry about shelling out premium prices ($47.00 or more) for some specific information that will help them solve the problem.

Speaking of premium prices, that reminds me of something I want to emphasize. At some point while writing your report, you will start getting sweaty palms as you think what seems to be a very scary thought...

"Oh crap, what if people realize all this information I have to share is available for FREE somewhere else?"

Relax. First of all, I challenge you to find me anything that isn't available somewhere for free. (Um, Libraries? Google? Wikipedia? Yahoo Answers? Hello!)

What you need to be concerned about is if it is available EASILY. For example, let's say as part of your HR job you taught a "lunch and learn" course on time management and you now want to take your notes and write up a report about it. You and I both know there is plenty of free time management information out there.

We could scour the internet, do google searches, check out some blogs and find 90% of this information without costing us a dime.

And that's exactly the problem.

People don't have time to scour! They don't want to *search* ...and then *click*...and then *read*...and then *decide* what's good versus what's total trash. Again, people want the INSTANT solution. They want someone who has done the research, taken the time to organize it and lay it out so that they can just get to the good stuff and run with it. They are willing to pay for speed and convenience. Just like at McDonald's.

Plus, with your time management information, if you put a mouth-watering title on it like: *10 Things Super-Busy Sales Managers Do To Free Up Time To Accomplish Awesome Stuff...* then you've just created a product targeted for a specific audience that is UNIQUE in the market place.

This is why my reports on *HR Blogging* and *Recession-Proofing Your HR Career* sold so well. It would take weeks for someone to gather up all this information by themselves. And by customizing it so that it spoke to a specific target audience (HR professionals), I enhanced its value even more. You should do the same thing.

'Nuff said. Let's move on.

5

STEP TWO: PINPOINTING HOT TOPICS YOU CAN BE SUCCESSFUL WITH ...INCLUDING 157 HR TOPIC IDEAS THAT YOU CAN STEAL, USE TODAY & PROFIT FROM

Now that you've selected your target audience, let's now focus in on your topic.

There are two basic rules for finding hot topics. But let me first caution you about a potential problem area that might sidetrack you if you're not prepared.

Let me say it this way...

Don't invest a <u>lot</u> of time in choosing a specific topic for your report.

This might seem to fly in the face of everything that I've said so far. But hold on, let me explain.

I'm not saying that you should make a stupid, rash, or **uninformed decision** as to what you should write about. On the contrary, I'm going to show you how to determine with *pinpoint accuracy* what is most likely to be a hot seller for you.

What I am saying is this: this is a SHORT report containing just 20 to 40 pages. It's not a full-length book. So, it isn't necessary that you spend months trying to find the ideal subject matter. You can crank these babies out over a few days. You're not trying to hit a home run here or create the next Amazon or New York Times best seller. You're simply looking for a topic that looks to be a winner to write a short special report about.

Don't miss the point here. The point is to QUICKLY create these short reports. You want...

Motion, not meditation.

There's not much risk here. So there's not much point in over-investing your time in any stage of this process.

Now, having said all of that, let's look at two criteria that I believe WILL allow you to quickly analyze the state of your market interest and determine what should prove to be a terrific topic for your next (or your first) report.

**CRITERIA #1:
DEMAND**

That is, there should be a significant amount of interest in a particular topic before you move forward. Obviously, the more interest there is in a topic, the more likely you'll be able to sell a report on it.

Now, the questions that I almost always get from folks are...

**How Can I Find Topics That Are In-Demand?
How Can I Judge "Demand" Or "Interest"
In A Particular Topic?**

Here are 6 different ways you can find topics that are "making a splash" within your particular market.

YOUR HR GOLDMINE

1. **Scan the best-sellers list as Amazon.com.** Do a search at Amazon.com (in the "books" section) for keywords and phrases that are related to your particular market. (i.e. "leadership" or "change management" or "labor relations") You should find a nice list of books ranked in order of popularity.

2. **Search Google to see what topics your "competition" has created products on.** Pay attention to those listed on the first page and those who are advertising in the ads on the right hand side of the screen. These will almost always provide you with numerous ideas for your report.

3. **Look in popular article directories for existing interest.** Drop by article banks such as GoArticles.com or EzineArticles.com and look at articles related to your market. Pay special attention to the "most viewed" articles as they are a good indicator of which topics are hot and which topics are not.

4. **Keep an eye out on Clickbank's Marketplace.** Clickbank (Clickbank.com/marketplace) is one of the largest sources of downloadable e-books, manuals and special reports online. The products that range in the top 5 positions within a particular category are usually selling very well...and they wouldn't be selling well if there wasn't interest! Look for categories in the marketplace that are related to your particular target audience and scan through the top 5-6 products listed. You're certain to find some great ideas for your report right there.

5. **Look in the HR forums for "Hot-Topics" that might lend themselves to report ideas.** There are forums (e.g. "message boards") for just about every group in HR imaginable. Look for discussions at these forums for ideas. Specifically, look for topics where there is a LOT of discussion (i.e. numerous posted messages and replies). Pay special attention for people who are complaining about problems or limitations

that you might be able to provide solutions for in your report.

6. **Find offline magazines related to your audience.** If your audience is other *"HR professionals,"* that's easy. Just look at the magazines you already read – i.e. *Workforce, HR Magazine, HR Executive* and the like. If your market is outside of HR, you'll need to do a bit more work. It starts with dropping by your favorite bookstore or newsstand (or visit Magazines.com online) and picking through their articles for short report ideas. This is another tremendous way to find great topic ideas - especially because you get the benefit of THEIR research. They've already invested time in deciding WHAT to write about based on their market's interest. You don't need to do this kind of research...simply write about what they are writing about...and add your own twist!

So, these are the six "idea hangouts" that will allow you to quickly judge demand for a topic before you write about it. By using these simple techniques, you should be able to brainstorm quite a few great topics for your special report.

With that in mind, let's address the second "criteria" for a hot-selling short report...

CRITERIA #2: SPECIFICITY

There needs to be something very SPECIFIC and DEFINITE about your report that makes it appealing to your target audience. The more precise you can be in your focus, the more likely it will be a hot seller. Remember, these are 20-40 page reports, so you need to finely focus your report on a precise topic.

Now, there are two options to consider in doing this...

Option 1: SEGMENT YOUR IDEA. In segmenting you idea, you take one smaller, specific piece of a larger topic and you explain it in great detail.

For example: You don't focus on a broad topic like "organization development." Instead, you focus on one piece of it, such as "using organization surveys to lower employee turnover." And you can even narrow that down even further to *"12 Quick, Easy And Low-Cost Ways To Use Organization Surveys To Lower Employee Turnover In Your Business."*

Let me give you a great hint here: Go to a sales page for an existing book or product related to your target audience. Look at their BULLET POINTS (these are benefit statements usually in a list of bullet points) and you should find some great "segments" to focus on.

Here's another example: Let's assume you want to create a short report that leverages your know-how on "talent management." To get some topics for your report, you can go to Amazon and look up books written on talent management, you might find one bullet point in the description of a book that says: *"How to quickly identify high potential talent without using time-consuming, complex assessments that most line managers hate."*

That one bullet point is a perfect topic for YOUR next report. It's a SEGMENT of "talent management". And when you position it properly (and we'll talk about how to do this later in this book), it could absolutely sell like crazy.

Option 2: SUPPLEMENT YOUR IDEA. In using the supplement option, you create a list of as many different ideas for one topic as you possibly can. Some examples for "talent management" might include...

- *17 Ways To Quickly Identify High Potential Talent Without Using Time-Consuming, Complex Assessments*
- *12 Ways To Increase The Number Of "Ready Now" Successors For Hard-To-Fill Leadership Positions*
- *10 Ways To Significantly Reduce The Time Required For Managers To Implement The Talent Review Process In Their Businesses*
- *15 Ways To Enforce Your Manager's Accountability For Growing Talent In Your Company Without Giving Them More Money.*

YOUR HR GOLDMINE

The idea is to give your reader as many possible ideas as you can think of. I've done this numerous times in the past with great success.

If you identify, let's say 20 *ways* or *ideas* for some particular topic, then you'd only need to write one page per idea to have a 20-page report. Simple!

People want to know as many different OPTIONS as are available. They think: "If I they can find at least one or two of these ideas to work for me and my situation, then it's probably worth it."

With a list of a variety of different ways, almost everyone finds something useful.

With these two criteria (demand and specificity) you should be able to quickly establish some great ideas for your next report. In fact, you should have a flood of ideas coming in. Spend half an hour brainstorming ideas. That should yield PLENTY of results.

Here Are A Couple Of Quick Additional Tips…

Save all of your ideas that you come up with by creating a "swipe file" containing them for future use. There's no need to go through this process again in 30 days when you already have the information at your fingertips. Additionally, as you are going through your regular HR day job routines, record any new great ideas that pop into your mind. These will be great options for future reports.

When you are developing your reports, think "series." If you can develop a general theme or a title that can be tweaked and duplicated over time, you should be able to get more customers to buy most (if not ALL) of your future installments. For example: Those who buy the *"Five Minute Guide for Using LinkedIn to Recruit Plant Managers"* will likely buy the *"Five Minute Guide for Using Twitter to Recruit Plant Managers"* and the *"Five Minute Guide for Using Facebook to Recruit Plant*

Managers". There's something magnetic about a "series" of similarly themed or titled reports.

Incidentally, in the above example, you could also substitute "Accountants" or "Engineers" for "Plant Managers." And create an entirely different line of reports for these categories.

BONUS:
A LIST OF 157 HR TOPIC IDEAS THAT YOU CAN STEAL, USE TODAY & PROFIT FROM

Many HR folks struggle to come up with a single viable topic idea for their special report. As a result, they get frustrated or they don't get going as fast as they could.

So, I've decided to include this bonus in this chapter. Here are 27 ideas for your next report, along with 157 title topics you can modify, steal or adapt for your own use. I'm sure that there is something on this list that can jump-start the selection of your next special report. But you be the judge. Here you go.

1. The How-To Tutorial.

Our list begins with the classic "how-to" report. This type of report is organized in a systematic, step-by-step, tutorial-style approach to accomplishing a task. The steps are most commonly organized in chronological order. (i.e. Step One is…, Step Two is…, etc.). These are generally known as "systems", "formulas", "checklists" or "blueprints". A few examples include…

1) *How to Stay Union-Free in 5 Easy Steps*
2) *How to Cut Employee Costs Without Layoffs in 10 Days*
3) *How to Retain The Gen X's in Your Workplace*
4) *How to Make Your First $1,000 as an HR Coach*
5) *How to Facilitate A Leadership Off-Site Meeting*
6) *How to Pass The SHRP Certification Exam The First Time*

2. Frequently Asked Questions

Another style of report is what I've labeled, "frequently asked questions". In this model, you would take 10-20 of the most asked questions about a particular topic and answer them in your content. This is one of the easiest kinds of short reports to create because outlining is simple due to the Q&A style. That is you just: (a) List the question and (b) Answer it.

While you'll want create better titles than the ones below, consider these just a few ideas for how this kind of report might be created...

7) *Top 20 Questions About Recruiting Engineers at Purdue*
8) *Top 20 Questions About Managing Large-Scale Change*
9) *Top 20 Questions About Improving Plant Productivity*
10) *Top 20 Questions About Finding Your Next Job in HR*
11) *Top 20 Questions About Work Life Balance*
12) *Top 20 Questions About Getting Promoted Faster*

3. The Interview

Moving from questions that YOU answer to questions that SOMEONE ELSE answers is another way to write a report. An *interview* report is, not surprisingly, a series of questions that you pose to one or more qualified experts to create the content you'll be selling.

Reasons why experts would do this for you include: free publicity for their web site, their career or business, rights to the completed report or paid compensation.

Again, these aren't *titles* for your report, but these are some things you might do for a handful of different topics...

13) Ask a headhunter questions about successful interviewing.
14) Ask a social media specialist about branding yourself online.

15) Ask a finance professional about financial metrics every HR personal should master.
16) Ask a consultant about starting up a consulting business.
17) Ask a senior executive about advice on getting promoted faster.

4. The List.

Another very popular kind of report is what I've labeled the "list." It is simply a listing of ways, strategies, tips, secrets, tactics, techniques, habits, exercises, principles, etc. with a detailed description of each entry to the list. Some examples of this kind of short report include...

18) *7 Ways To Get Hiring Managers To Read Your Resume*
19) *5 Little Known Strategies For Retaining Engineers*
20) *50 Best Practices For Getting & Staying Organized*
21) *10 Advantages You Need To Avoid Getting Laid Off*
22) *Top 10 Time Management Tips You've NEVER Been Told About*

5. The Case Study

Next on our list of types of short reports is the "case study" model. This would consist of you profiling different successful examples of people accomplishing a common task. In other words, you'd show how several different achievers (including or not including yourself) have reached the desired result. The great thing about this kind of report the variety of different methods people use in attaining similar results. Your readers will likely *connect* with one or more of the examples and get a sense of motivation and empowerment to reach their goal as well. Bottom line: you've got a satisfied customer. A few examples include (these are ideas, not titles)...

23) *Learn The Biggest Obstacles 7 Gay Engineers Overcame To Become Corporate Vice Presidents*

YOUR HR GOLDMINE

24) *The Employee Engagement Secrets of 7 Most Profitable Small Businesses*
25) *Talent Management Practices of the 10 Fastest Growing Small Businesses*
26) *10 Employee On-boarding Programs You Can Legally "Steal" And Use Immediately In Your Organization*

6. The Resource Directory

The next kind of short report is the "resource directory." That is, a group of related people, companies or resources (usually indexed categorically and then alphabetically) along with their contact information such as web site, phone number and or mailing/physical address. A few examples of this kind of report would include...

27) *The Midwest Guide To HR Consultants & Search Firms*
28) *The HR Professional's Guide To The Best Talent Management Software*
29) *The Labor Negotiator's Resource Guide To The Teamsters*
30) *The Organization Assessment & Survey Source Book*
31) *The 101 Most Fun, Quick "Team Building" Ice-Breakers*
32) *The Top 50 Recommended iPhone Apps for HR Pros*

7. Idea Generators

Up next we have the "idea generators" style of report. This particular kind of report is a best described as a collection of ideas to help the reader accomplish a goal. Here are a few different examples...

33) *21 Quick Ideas For Improving Workforce Productivity*
34) *75 Revealing Questions To Ask In Your Next Interview*
35) *97 Winning Ideas To Kickoff Your Next Off-site Meeting*
36) *10 Ideas For Quickly Reducing Workplace Accidents*
37) *10 Fill-In-The-Blank Templates for Formatting Resumes*

YOUR HR GOLDMINE

38) *The Ultimate List of Ideas for Managing Change*

8. The First Year

Up next is what I've labeled "the first year". In this kind of report, you'd walk a newcomer through the first 12 months of a particular endeavor. What beginner standing on the threshold of something completely new to them wouldn't want the wisdom of what to expect and how to successfully navigate through the foundation period?

You could chronicle the first year with a calendar of milestones and guideposts, pitfalls to avoid, shortcuts to take and so forth. Some examples are...

39) *The First Year as a New HR Leader*
40) *The First Year as a New Consultant*
41) *The First Year of Life In the Workforce After College*
42) *The First Year as an Expat in the U.S.*
43) *The First Year of Life After Being Downsized*
44) *The First Year of Coming Out as a Gay Employee*
45) *The First Year as a Comp & Benefits Specialist*
46) *The First Year of Retirement*

9. Niche Business

One of the biggest mistakes that most HR professionals make is trying to create information products to sell to large, well-known corporations. It's a cycle that just loops over and over again. Fortunately for you, there's another option. Instead of selling your HR expertise to the big fish, teach the little minnows...i.e. small "niche" business owners about HR. ALL business owners, regardless of what their business is, need to know how to get the most and best out of their employees.

Note: What's interesting about this kind of report is the fact that you can make a few changes and "niche it" for numerous different topics (e.g. *"The Bookstore Owner's Guide to Hiring Smart," "The Real Estate Agent's Guide to Hiring Smart," "The*

Hair Salon Owner's Guide to Hiring Smart", etc.). Here are some additional examples…

47) The Christian Bookstore Owner's Guide To Employee Job Sharing
48) The Pet Store Owner's Guide To Correcting Employee Performance Problems
49) The Personal Trainer's Guide To Avoiding Sexual Harassment Complaints
50) How To Terminate Real Estate Agents Without Litigation
51) A Crash Course in Health Care Plans For Independent Singers
52) Workplace Protections You Need To Know About For Employing Foreign Workers In Your Construction Business

10. The Bridge

I've labeled this next kind of short report "the bridge." The idea is to bridge universal wants and needs related to HR (i.e. how to interview, how to get a job, ask your boss for a raise, position yourself for a promotion, have great work relationships, etc.) into different occupational groups and customize a report specifically for them. Some examples are…

53) The Engineer's Guide To Getting Promoted
54) The Plant Manager's Guide For Building Teams
55) The GenY Guide To Career Advancement
56) The Teacher's Guide to Interviewing Successfully
57) Finding Talented Employees on a Small Budget For Small Business Owners
58) The Work at Home Mom's Guide To Finding A New Job

11. Shortcuts

Who among us wouldn't like to take shortcuts (assuming they don't have drawbacks) to achieve a desired result faster, easier or better? The short answer is: no one. With this kind of report you would focus on ways to save time or effort in accomplishing a specific task without sacrificing any benefits or quality. Some examples are...

59) *17 Shortcuts For Reducing Employee Turnover*
60) *10 Shortcuts To Mastering Any Job In 30 Days or Less*
61) *Top 10 Shortcuts For Mastering PeopleSoft®*
62) *5 Simple Shortcuts For Acing The HR Certification Exam*
63) *7 Shortcuts For Crafting The Perfect HR Strategy*
64) *Shortcuts For Employee Surveys: How To Execute Them Faster, Easier and Better*

12. Advanced Guide

To an extent we've already talked about focusing your report on "beginners" (See #8: "The First Year"), but what about those who have an elevated state of experience or knowledge? There is a huge market for "advanced" information in just about every field. So, creating a short report focused on providing information for the experienced or advanced user is another great idea.

Note: To create a great one-two punch, why not write a "beginners" report on a topic and then create an "advanced" report on the same topic. Then, you are able to graduate your beginners to the advanced report after they've read the first one. Some examples are...

65) *The Advanced Guide For Using Social Media in HR*
66) *Advanced Coaching Skills For the HR Executive*
67) *Advanced Job Search Strategies For People in Transition*
68) *15 Tips & Strategies For The Advanced Group Facilitator*
69) *Seven Advanced Positive Labor Relations Strategies For The Food Industry*
70) *Advanced Headhunting: 12 Ways To Recruit Anyone, Anywhere, Anytime!*

13. Time Frame

With this kind of short report you would focus most of your positioning on the TIME FRAME in which the task can be completed. Everything would be structured towards seeing results within a specific period of time; that would be the selling point. More important than getting results is knowing how long it's going to take to get those results (assuming it's not long! ☺).

Case Study: Jan Wallen created a report (that later became a book) entitled, *Mastering LinkedIn in 7 Days or Less*. There were NUMEROUS reports and books available at the time about LinkedIn, but hers was the first that emphasized a specific time frame. The point: You can sell the same topic to a crowded marketplace if you stress a time period! Some examples are…

71) *How To Cut Your HR Budget by 10% in 10 Days.*
72) *The 7-Day Plan for Creating A New Employee Orientation Program*
73) *Find Your Next Job in 30 Days or Less*
74) *Pass the HR Certification Exam in 21 Days or Less*
75) *Get Up To Speed in Your New HR Job In 2 Weeks Or Less*

14. Personal Profile

What's more likely to get your attention: an overweight friend who says "I've got some great information on losing weight" or a thin friend who used to be overweight who says "let me show you how I lost the weight?" Obviously unless you're suffering from delirium, the thin friend gets your vote. Why? Because when we see that someone has achieved the results we'd like to achieve, there is credibility.

By creating a report that reveals and explains how you accomplished a specific task that others want to accomplish you should have an instant hit on your hands. In this kind of short report, simply chronicle what you did. Some examples are…

76) *How I Went From HR Admin to HR Manager in 12 Months -- And How You Can Too!*
77) *How I Got A 7% Merit Increase When No One Else Did.*
78) *How I Convinced My Reluctant Boss To Pay For My MBA.*
79) *How I Convinced the CEO To Become My Mentor.*
80) *How I Wrote A Book While I Kept My Full-Time HR Job.*
81) *How I Kept My Job While Everyone Else In My Department Lost Theirs*

15. Planner

Some of the most popular short reports ever have been "planners". For our purposes, a planner is simply a set of activities arranged in a daily schedule as a sort of checklist to work through. Why do people love them? Because it allows them to stay on track. They see a set of action steps to complete for Monday, then Tuesday, then Wednesday and so forth. Most people find it much easier to actually do something when it's arranged in this kind of order.

Note: This is one of my top recommendations for a report. Every report author should write at least one of these "planners" to sell online. Some examples are...

82) *The 7-Day Checklist For Reducing Absenteeism*
83) *The 31-Day Guide To Running an Employee Survey*
84) *The 7-Day Guide To Becoming an HR Consultant*
85) *The 4-Week Guide To Surviving a Corporate Merger*
86) *The Smart HR Executive's Daily Schedule*
87) *33 Days To Winning a Union Organizing Campaign*

16. What To Do When

This is another classic example of the "problem/solution" format. It's just expressed in a different way. The idea here is to inform the reader what they should do when they find themselves facing a specific problem that can still be remedied.

YOUR HR GOLDMINE

A key is to focus on a narrow and very specific issue in your title.

To be clear: It's not, *What To Do Get Your Dream Job,* but rather *What To Do When You Are A Finalist For Your Dream Job.* Some examples are...

88) *What To Do When You're A Finalist For Your Dream Job (*no sense in wasting a good title!)
89) *What To Do When Your Mentor Isn't Giving You Good Advice*
90) *What To Do When Your Very Best Employee Wants To Quit*
91) *What To Do When You Worry Too Much About Office Politics*
92) *What To Do When You've Not Prepared For A Critical Management Presentation*
93) *What To Do When You Can't Get Promoted and You've Tried Everything*

17. Pop Culture Lessons

This kind of report is for the creative writer. If you're not creative, then feel free to move on to #18. ☺ The idea here is to share lessons that you've gleaned from pop culture. (i.e. movies, music, lifestyles, fashion, entertainment, cooking, etc.)

One of the reasons why this is usually a very good seller is because of its inherent ability to create curiosity.

What recruiter wouldn't be interested to learn how watching *American Idol* can help them pick great job candidates?

What general manager wouldn't want to know Santa Claus' "low cost" secrets of maximizing the performance of the elves in his/her business?

The point is, there are built-in opportunities to grab attention (and get sales!) by including pop culture lessons as the focus of your report. Some examples are...

94) 10 Awesome HR Business Presentation Lessons From The Academy Awards
95) What I Learned From Victoria Secret About Getting Along With Powerful Business Women
96) The American Idol Fan's Guide To Building Great Relationships at Work
97) The Survivor Success Model For Acing Your Next Performance Review
98) How To Turn "You're Fired" Into "You're Hired"
99) Everything I Know About Mentoring I Learned From Shrek

18. Current Events Tie-In

Another great idea for your next short report is to tie-in the content to an upcoming holiday or event. The reason this is such an effective report is because it has a natural "urgency" trigger. In other words, the potential customer needs to buy your report NOW in order to reap the benefits by the imposed deadline (i.e. the date of the event or holiday). Some examples are…

100) How To Accomplish All Your Annual Performance Objectives Before Spring Break
101) 17 Ways To Save Money On Christmas Gifts For Your Employees
102) How To Take The Summer Vacation Of Your Dreams …And Attend The Top Leadership Conference On the Planet For Free
103) How To Land An Outstanding Speaker for Your Local SHRM Annual Conference Convention
104) 10 Ways To Reduce Employee Expenses (Without Laying Off One Single Employee) Before April 15th
105) The Last-Minute Guide For Planning A Great Employee Picnic at Your Company's Anniversary Celebration

19. Save Money

The idea here is to create a short report that teaches the reader how to save money or completely eliminate the cost that is associated with a particular activity.

Think about the appeal of this particular kind of report...

**You're offering the reader the opportunity
to reduce (sometimes GREATLY reduce) the costs
associated with something they are going to do anyway!**

Who wouldn't pay $10 for your report if it's going to save them $200, $500, $1000 or even more? Who wouldn't pay $10 for your short report if it's going to allow them to reduce their costs EVERY TIME they complete a particular task or participate in a specific activity? Two words for you: gold mine. Some examples...

> 106) *How To Tap Into a Little-Known Resource That Will Save You At Least 25% On All Your Office Expenses*
> 107) *How To Win 97% of All Your Workers Compensation Claims*
> 108) *7 "Tricks" For Getting Any Management Consultant or Headhunter To Lower Their Asking Price*
> 109) *How To Lower The Cost of Your Next Out-of-Town HR Offsite Meeting by 60%*
> 110) *14 Ways To Reduce The Costs of Employee Training That You'll Already Budgeted For*
> 111) *Don't Get Burned: 5 Sure-Fire Ways To Save Money On Your Next HR Information System (HRIS).*

20. Make Money

Just the opposite of #19 is teaching people how to "make money" doing something they are already going to do anyway. Who wouldn't be interested in generating cash doing something they enjoy? Who wouldn't want to get paid to do something they are already going to do?

Two more words for you: gold mine.

When you find a passion of your target audience and then deliver a short report that teaches them how to make money from that passion or how to turn it into a business, you're certain to have a hit on your hands. Some examples are...

112) *How To Make Money as a Part-Time Consultant While Still Working at Your Day Job*
113) *How To Make Money Selling All Those Work-Related Books on Your Shelves for Top Prices on Ebay®*
114) *How To Get Paid For Giving Talks on Your HR Expertise -- Even If You Aren't Today Published, Polished or Established!*
115) *The Human Resources Professional's Guide To Making Money in Photography By Taking Photos of Unusual People.*
116) *How To Turn Your HR Job Into A Consulting Business*
117) *How To Publish Your Own Blog on Your HR Specialty For Fun And Profit!*

21. Faster and Easier

Another kind of report is what I've labeled "faster and easier." The idea here is to position your report as a resource that reveals information that enables the reader to accomplish some task faster and/or easier than they were previously able to do. Some examples are...

118) *The Fastest & Easiest Way To Recruit on Twitter*
119) *The Easiest Way To Get Applicants To Your Company's Web Site*
120) *Seven Faster & Easier Ways To Improve Your Diversity Hiring Results*
121) *Five Simple Strategies For Achieving Your Performance Objectives Faster*

122) How To Skip A Few Rungs As You Climb The Corporate Ladder

22. Barriers & Mistakes

With virtually any pursuit in life there are potential pitfalls and common blunders associated with that pursuit. The old adage is, "an ounce of prevention is worth a pound of cure" and there is some truth to that. A properly positioned report highlighting barriers and mistakes (and how to avoid them!) would be another great option for you to consider. Some examples are:

123) 7 Common Mistakes Made in Utilizing Facebook in HR ...And How To Avoid Them
124) 10 Most Common Mistakes in Managing GenX Employees -- And How To Fix Them
125) How To Overcome The 7 Biggest Barriers That All New HR Leaders Face
126) The 10 Hidden Barriers To Communicating Persuasively That No One Told You About
127) 7 Barriers To Productive Work Relationships–And How To Overcome Them
128) 5 Big Barriers To Improving Employee Absenteeism

Note: Your sales message is very important for this kind of special report. You'll want to stress how easy it is to make mistakes and what kind of disadvantage the reader will face if they don't apply the strategies you share in your report.

23. Turn It Into

It's almost like magic: take something you've already got and "turn it into" something much more desirable. That's the idea behind this kind of report. It's presented in the classic "how-to" format (i.e. arranged in chronological steps). Some examples are:

YOUR HR GOLDMINE

129) How To Turn An Interview Into A Job
130) How To Turn Your HR Know-How Into A Thriving Coaching Business
131) How To Turn Your Boss Into Your Biggest Advocate
132) How To Turn Your Worst Enemy Into Your Most Trusted Colleague
133) How To Turn Your Worst Performing Manufacturing Plant into the Gold Standard for Your Organization
134) How To Turn Your HR Department Into A Profit Center

24. The 5-Minute Guide To

The concept of "5-minutes" carries several highly desirable elements to it:

(a) Relief to a problem that can be gained in just a few minutes.
(b) Slight changes that bring desirable results which can be made in just a few minutes.
(c) An overview or "working knowledge" of a process that can be learned in just a few minutes.

With so many of life's activities, we'd like the "readers digest" version – that is, we just want to know, in as few words as possible, how to do it. Some examples are…

135) The 5-Minute Guide To Managing Top Talent
136) The 5-Minute Guide To Addressing Performance Issues
137) The 5-Minute Guide To Improving Productivity
138) The 5-Minute Guide To Being A Leader
139) The 5-Minute Guide To Influencing Others
140) The 5-Minute Guide To Organizing Your Work Life

25. Survival

There are times in life when, quite frankly, a solution to a problem isn't possible. All layoffs can't be avoided, all EEO lawsuits aren't won, and all employee injuries can't be avoided. Sometimes difficult times do come and they must be dealt with. In the "survival" type of short report you would teach your readers how to deal with a problem that they cannot avoid. Some examples are:

141) How To Survive Losing an EEO Case and Learn To Trust Your Company (or Another One) Again
142) How To Survive A Big Pay Cut And Rebound Financially
143) How To Survive Being Laid Off And Move Forward in Your Career Without Fear
144) How To Survive The Loss of Your Top Employee Without Lowering Morale or Productivity
145) How To Survive Suing Your Company Without Destroying Your Career or Your Relationships at Work
146) How To Survive A Painful Demotion and Keep Your Head Held High

26. Top Picks

With so much information available, it can become difficult knowing what's best. That's why a "top picks" kind of short report is another solid idea for you to develop.

Stated simply, you would give your opinion as to what the top picks are within your topic. Obviously, it's all about your how you position the content. There's a big difference between these two report titles...*7 Places To Take Find Top Talent In New England* and *7 Little-Known Sources For Finding Top Talent in New England Almost No One Knows About*

Two words come to mind when I think of this option: Consumer Reports®. They are incredibly popular because people want an unbiased review and recommendation for something they are considering buying. Some examples are...

147) *Seven Little-Known Sources For Finding Top Talent in Chicago Almost No One Knows About*
148) *How To Spend A $2000 HR Budget For Max Results*
149) *The 3 Best Ways To Build Leadership Skills on a Low-Cost Budget*

150) The Top 15 Tips For Getting Candidate Traffic To Any Corporate Career Site
151) The Top 10 Ways To Find Anything on Anyone Online Before You Hire Them

27. Age Specific

The final idea I want to share for you to consider as an option for your next report is simply what I'm going to label as "age specific."

What you would do is develop a short report on a specific topic for a specific age group. Let's face it, you wouldn't deal with a teenager the same way you would a senior citizen. Different ages require different approaches, which makes this a wonderful way for you to niche your report (and, in many cases, continue to "graduate" your customers from one report to the next as they or someone they know continues to grow older). Some examples are...

152) 12 Career Reinvention Strategies for Baby Boomers.
153) How To Retire By Age 35 And Never Work Again
154) The Age 50+ Guide To Getting Hired in the Fortune 100
155) How To Manage & Get The Most From Your GenX Employees
156) 7 Strategies Large Companies Utilize To Re-engage Their Retirees in Their Business Without Re-employing Them...and How You Can Too!
157) The New Employee's Guide to Mastering Performance Appraisals.

Closing Thoughts

So, there you have it...27 different ideas for your next short report with 157 title topics you can modify for your own use. If you combine all this with the selection criteria covered at the beginning of this chapter, you should have an ample number of starting points for your first or your next short report!

6

STEP THREE: PREPARING P.A.G.E.S. OF COMPELLING INFORMATION THAT PEOPLE ARE HUNGRY FOR NOW

In this chapter, I'm going to walk you through how to prepare your 20-40 page report in a way that will compel readers to buy it.

But, before we begin with that, let me briefly say a word about how to "title" your reports.

Keep this in mind from the beginning…

The <u>TITLE</u> is the SINGLE MOST IMPORTANT factor in converting browsers into buyers and generating extra income from your special reports.

In other words, it's critical that your title be something more appealing than, *"Susan's Guide to Labor Relations"*. ☺

If the title of your report doesn't make a BOLD PROMISE that literally jerks you reader out of their chair and grabs them by the throat, they'll never want to read it. It's just that simple.

Here's why.

YOUR HR GOLDMINE

These days, it takes a pretty good title to capture the eyeballs of busy readers who are time-strapped and constantly scanning scores if not hundreds of web pages every day.

So you have to hook 'em. You can't hesitate to use catchy, witty, edgy, attention-grabbing titles that will at least get your readers to scan a description of your report to learn more.

While there are numerous criteria that you might want to consider in choosing a title, I've narrowed them down to what I consider to be the three most important considerations. As the old Jackson Five song goes: "it's easy as A,B,C…"

A. **Does the title "Accurately represent"?** In other words, does your title mention "specifically" what's included in the report? *"The HR Certification Guide,"* isn't specific. *"How to Pass The HR Certification Exam"* is narrowing it down better, but isn't nearly as accurate or specific as *"21 Shortcuts For Passing the HR Certification Exam."*

B. **Does the title "Build interest"?** That is, is your report title *"appealing",* even *"enticing"*? Your title should, in itself, begin to create a desire to purchase the report. *"How to Pass the HR Certification Exam"* isn't nearly as appealing and intriguing as *"21 Little-Known Shortcuts I Used To Pass The HR Certification Exam on the First Try – That You Can Use Too!"*

C. **Does the title "Communicate benefits"?** That is, when someone reads the title of your report, do they have a reasonable expectation of some desirable result they can achieve by purchasing, reading and applying your report? Reports that scream ULTIMATE BENEFIT are the most appealing, simply because we are emotional creatures. We want something that is going to deliver the desired result we are after. And if the title communicates that it can deliver that result, we will definitely take a closer look.

For example: *"Searching For Brand Manager Jobs Using LinkedIn"* doesn't offer nearly the benefit that *"Using Lin-*

YOUR HR GOLDMINE

kedIn To Find Your Next Brand Manager Job In 30 Days!" does. Note the difference: One says "search" the other says "find." Brand managers who are out of work want to find jobs, not search for them. Also in the first example, it doesn't promise when. The other says "In 30 Days!" Catch the distinction?

For report titles, if you use the A-B-C approach that I just gave you, you can create some magnetic titles. In most cases, a simple "*How To*" title will work best. Occasionally, depending upon what you're writing, what I call a *"numerical"* title will work well. The follow are examples of this kind of title:
- *"21 Ways to Keep Your Organization Union-Free"*
- *"7 Strategies Any Leader Can Use To Cut Their People Costs Without Downsizing"*
- *"The One Secret Way You Can Determine If You're About To Be Laid Off"*

Okay, let's move on. After establishing some criteria for the title of your report, let's talk now about content.

Here is a simple five-step formula that you can use for creating lengthier pieces of content (i.e. reports and other "how-to" information products) which has rarely been shared before in the format I'm about to give to you.

It's called "P.A.G.E.S," which is simply an acronym which stands for:

P - PLAN out your report by brainstorming ideas.
A - ARRANGE your ideas sequentially or systematically.
G - GROW your content by "filling in the blanks."
E - EXTRACT bullet points for your ad copy as you write.
S - SMOOTH out the rough spots to complete the report.

I'll now walk you through how to put each of these five parts of the P.A.G.E.S. formula into action so you can quickly and easily create your own 20-40 page reports.

STEP #1:
PLAN OUT YOUR REPORT BY BRAINSTORMING IDEAS.

Obviously, by this time, you should have chosen your topic. So, where do you go from there? You start by simply brainstorming ideas for possible inclusion in your report. The easiest way that I've discovered for doing this is to simply...

Write a list of everything you want to share.

That's right, just write down everything. I'm talking about just rambling on paper (or on your computer screen). Everything you can think of that relates to the subject of your report. Just a list of "ideas" you want to share.

Don't worry about relevance or whether or not you'll even use all of these ideas. Just get them down. Jot down as many of these as you can find...

- Ideas
- Notes
- Lists
- Questions
- Reminders
- Personal reflections
- Thoughts
- Things-To-Do
- Checklists
- Details
- Steps
- Facts
- Reasons
- Comparisons
- Contrasts
- Statistics
- Quotes
- Illustrations

YOUR HR GOLDMINE

- Stories

Write down everything you can think of or can find during your research.

Don't worry about whether or not it makes sense. Don't worry about how well it's written. Don't worry that it doesn't fit with anything else. Just write capture everything you can related to the topic of your report.

Now, I want to give you one of the most invaluable brainstorming exercises you'll ever use for generating ideas for your report. I call it "alphabetizing".

Starting with the letter "A" in the alphabet, literally begin thinking of events, places, people, items, verbs, ideas, etc. that begin with that letter and are related to the topic of your report. The goal is to go all the way to "Z". This is a great way to brainstorm ideas.

FOR EXAMPLE: If you are creating a product related to the qualities needed by front-line supervisors to excel on the job during tough times, you might have...

> A = Adaptability
> B = Belief
> C = Communications
> D = Dependability
> E = Empathy
> F = Focus
> G = Guidance

After you've gotten keywords for each of the 26 letters of the alphabet, jot down any notes about each of those entries that you want to mention in your report. And just like that you've got 26 ideas to write about in your report. If you just wrote 1/4 page on each of them, you'd have almost 7 pages of content!

So, that's how you "*plan out your report by brainstorming ideas*". That's the "P" of the "P.A.G.E.S." system. Now, let's move on to...

STEP #2:
ARRANGE YOUR IDEAS SEQUENTIALLY OR SYSTEMATICALLY.

This step doesn't require a lot of explanation, but let me go ahead and just touch on this a bit just for clarification. There are two basic ways to "arrange" your ideas once you have them all jotted down - in other words "organize" them so they make sense. These two ways are to do it "sequentially" and "systematically."

Sequentially...
That is, organizing your ideas in chronological steps. In providing any kind of "how-to" solution there is a logical order in which steps occur. You would simply outline your report based on what comes first and then what comes after that. Step 1 is... Step 2 is... Step 3 is... Now, as a rule of thumb, I recommend that you keep the total number of steps to something in SINGLE DIGITS. No more than 9 steps. Anything more than that could be viewed as "too much work" in the eyes of your readers. So, organize all of your ideas in 9 or less steps, beginning with the step that comes first and ending with the step that comes last.

Systematically...
The other option is to organize things "systematically". In other words, you'd group ideas together based on their logical relationship to each other.

Example 1: If your title is "*5 Keys to Getting Promoted Now,*" then that's the basic framework for your outline. You divide things into sections or parts, one for each of the 5 Keys. Key #1 is a section. Key #2 is a section. And so forth. All of your ideas would fall into one of your 5 Keys.

Example 2: If you have a LOT of different ideas, such as "*101 Low-Cost Ways For Recognizing, Rewarding & Retaining Top Talent,*" then find 5-9 main topics to group them into. For example: "Awards & Trophies," "Fun Freebies," "Special Recognition Events," "Senior Management Involvement" and so forth.

Note: Now, let me give you a recommendation on arranging ideas that I've found to be very important over the years. While you want ALL of your short reports to contain quality content that's useful to your customer, let's face it, some points are stronger than others. There are some things you'll be sharing that are just better or more important or less known than others. It's important that you fire these FIRST and LAST. That is, you want your best work to be in the first few pages and then finish strong in the last few pages. If you have any content that's "weaker" than the rest, then you'll want to include it somewhere in the middle if it's important enough to share at all. It's not that you're trying to "hide" anything, it's simply that you want to minimize your weaknesses and showcase your strengths. (The exception to this rule is a report where you lay out sequential steps. Understandably, these "steps" should be presented in whatever order they appear in the sequence.)

That same rule of thumb can be used with any "sub-ideas" you have for each of your main points (your "ways" or "steps", etc.). Your strongest sub-ideas come first and last with the others mixed in the middle somewhere.

And with that, we're on to....

STEP #3:
GROW YOUR CONTENT BY "FILLING IN THE BLANKS."

At this point you should have a nice outline created from all of your ideas. Now, it's simply a matter of "filling in the blanks". That is, writing a few paragraphs of meaty information for each of the points listed in your outline. That's all it takes. (You should have at least 26 "points" listed from the alphabetizing exercise.) Remember, you're only striving to create 20-40 pages of quality information.

You just need to do a little math. You take the total number of pages that you want and divide it by the total number of ideas that you've written down so you can see how much you need to write for each point.

Example: Let's suppose you want to create a 20 page report on your topic. Let's further suppose that you have 40 "ideas" that you've brainstormed to share in the report that you have arranged in 5 different sections. Doing the math, we find that you need 1/2 page of content per idea in order to meet the page requirement. So, you just begin writing the first point and when you reach 1/2 page, you know you can quit anytime you finalize the thought you're sharing.

Some of your points will require less space to share than the numbers would demand. That's okay, because some of your points will go over. It all balances out in the end, and it's not an exact science. It's just a way to keep things balanced.

It really doesn't even matter that you do the math...as long as you do the writing. Simply write a few paragraphs explanation for each of the points. Don't be afraid to mix in some humor. Inject your own personality into the writing.

Now, what I want to do for you before we move on to the next steps is to share some "content templates" with you that will also help you create content for your report.

Here's how it works. I'm going to provide you with five content templates. Each one consists of an opening sentence that you can apply to any portion of your product where you might need some additional ideas for content.

Content Template #1: *"If I could sum up <blank> in <blank> steps, here is what they would be…"*

Where you see the "<blank>" you just fill them in with whatever topic you're going to be discussing in that section of your report.

For example: *"If I could sum up my philosophy of **leading successful team meetings** in 3 steps, here is what they would be…"*

Elaborating further, you might say...
    Step 1: Set a clear agenda in advance.
    Step 2: Ensure the meeting stays on track.
    Step 3: Capture the key decisions and next steps.

So, you begin a section by opening with the above sentence by completing the blank sections with whatever topic you plan on discussing in that section.

Here are some other examples:
- *"If I could sum up **how to create an inclusive workplace for LGBTs** in 5 steps, here is what they would be..."*
- *"If I could sum up **HR's role in mergers & acquisitions** in 4 steps, here is what they would be..."*
- *"If I could sum up **what makes up an effective onboarding program for new college grads** in 3 steps, here is what they would be..."*
- *"If I could sum up how to **develop a vision statement** in 5 steps, here is what they would be..."*

Your opening sentence sets the stage for that section. Just insert your own topic in the template and you're ready to begin. Next, you write supporting paragraphs for each of the three steps, which can be as little as one paragraph, but should be preferably 3-4 paragraphs per step.

Content Template #2: *"One of the things that the majority of folks find most challenging about <blank> is <blank>..."*

For example: *"One of the things that the majority of folks find most challenging about **time management** is **handling interruptions.**"*

Some other examples might include...
- *"One of the things that the majority of folks find most challenging about **consulting** is **working without a steady paycheck.**"*
- *"One of the things that the majority of folks find most challenging about **labor relations** is **negotiating union contracts.**"*
- *"One of the things that the majority of folks find most challenging about **downsizing the workforce** is to **communicating the news to the impacted employees.**"*

- *"One of the things that the majority of folks find most challenging about **purchasing a new payroll system** is **making certain they get the best price**."*

In using a template like this one, I'd first briefly describe the challenge itself. Why is it so difficult? What problems do most folks face when attempting to do it? What makes it challenging? Then I'd spend 2-3 paragraphs describing the challenge itself. Then, suggest a solution. Yep, you've got the answers. And you're willing to share them. So, offer some advice on how to overcome the challenge. Outline 4 or 5 tips for solving the problem. Each tip only needs to be 1 paragraph in length, but it all adds up to a great deal of content.

Content Template #3: *"A little known secret about <blank> is <blank>"*

Some variations on this theme include...
- A seldom used tactic
- An often misunderstood approach
- An often overlooked technique
- The best kept secret for
- One of the most powerful ways

Some examples might be:
- *"A little known secret about **selling your ideas** is to **NEVER forget to link them to your client's needs**."*
- *"A little known secret about **designing new compensation programs** is to **also include ways of providing non-monetary recognition**."*
- *"A little known secret about **managing an HR budget** is to **allocate dollars for entertainment**"*
- *A little known secret about **developing a strategic planning document** is to **not forget to include a one-page executive summary**."*

Content Template #4: *"Perhaps one of the biggest reasons that people fail in <blank> is <blank>"*

Examples would include:
- *"Perhaps one of the biggest reasons that people fail in **assuming a new job** is **a lack of training**."*
- *"Perhaps one of the biggest reasons that people fail in **managing their HR budget** is **they underestimate recruitment costs**."*
- *"Perhaps one of the biggest reasons that people fail in **managing their time** is **a lack of discipline**."*
- *"Perhaps one of the biggest reasons that people fail in **managing conflict** is **they use the wrong approach**."*

After exposing what is perhaps the biggest reason that people fail in achieving their desired outcome, give the reader several quick tips on how to avoid failure, specifically mentioning how to achieve success.

See how easy this is when you just have a starting point?

You could probably easily work in 4 or 5 tips about achieving success in a particular area.

You could probably weave in a short 3-5 step system for achieving success in a particular area.

You could probably pose and answer several questions relating to success in a particular area.

It's all about having something to begin with, which is the purpose of our content templates here.

Content Template #5: *"The one thing I always get asked about <blank> is <blank>."*

Some examples might be:
- *"The one thing I always get asked about **performance appraisal programs** is **how many rating categories should be used**."*
- *"The one thing I always get asked about **diversity** is **how do you best include white males**."*
- *"The one thing I always get asked about **conflict management** is **how to keep from getting angry**."*
- *"The one thing I always get asked about **union organizing drives** is **what can I do to avoid them altogether**."*

Fire away your most asked question and then answer it. Provide your reader with as many tips or steps in your answer as you can.

So, those are the five content templates. Plug in your responses and you're off and running.

Now, let's move on to...

STEP #4:
EXTRACT BULLET POINTS FOR YOUR AD COPY WHILE YOU WRITE.

In an upcoming chapter, I'm going to share with you how to write a "sales message" to convince your target audience to buy your report. What is going to be invaluable to you in that part of the process is what you do right here in step four of your content creation.

With any good sales message, there will be a "bullet list" of benefit statements. I'm sure you've seen them in many sales messages online. They offer encapsulated glimpses into what the product or service being offered means in terms of its benefit to you.

What I like to do is develop these bullet points as I'm writing the content. Over and over again, I've found myself writing things in my reports like, "the fastest way I know to..." or "3 of the easiest ways to..." or "my own secret weapon for..." or "if you don't do anything else, make sure you do this..."

So, when I find myself writing these phrases, I stop at the completion of my thought process and write down a variation of that statement to later use as a bullet point in my sales message.

To illustrate, here are some example bullet points taken from my HR Recession Guide report:

- *The 7 strategies that work <u>best</u> in the current economy if you want to keep your job and build and your HR career. (Note: While no one can guarantee you that your job will be safe, these strategies greatly enhance your chances of success.)*

- *What even the most talented Human Resources professionals are <u>NOT</u> doing which is putting their job and their career at risk.*
- *Which HR career strategies used to work in the 1990s and early 2000s, but are now <u>obsolete</u> and simply not effective in this recession.*
- *How just being <u>busy doing your HR job</u> can be a fatal career mistake and make your job even more vulnerable to being eliminated.*
- *Extra Bonus! What you should do right now if you are absolutely convinced that you are about to be let go, and it's too late and there's nothing you can do about it. Here are the action steps you should take immediately before the ax falls!*

Notice, of course, that they are in bullet form. ☺

You'll want to follow this practice too as you're writing your report. Just take a few seconds to extract statements that you can use as persuasive bulleted benefits in your marketing. I recommend that you grab about 10-12 of them for the sales page that you'll create later.

And now, let's cover the final step...

STEP #5:
<u>S</u>MOOTH OUT THE ROUGH SPOTS TO COMPLETE YOUR REPORT.

Once you've written the content for your report, you'll want to fine-tune it. Generally speaking, there are three things that I recommend you do in putting on the finishing touches for your report...

- <u>PAD</u>. That is, look for areas of your report that need further explanation. Are there any areas that are not clearly explained? Are there areas that are noticeably weaker than others? Make sure your points are understandable. Try to add in as many examples as possible to better illustrate the points. Toss in a few more tips here and there

where needed. You can add interviews, transcripts, quotes, research and other bits of information to get the points across better and add a bit more meat to the report.
- <u>POLISH</u>. Use different fonts to distinguish areas of your content. Change colors. Use alternative styles such as bold face, italics and underline. Indent text where appropriate. Use bullet points (especially on lists.) Insert headers, footers and graphics (just don't overdo it!) Make your short report look special! (We'll talk more about this in our next section.)
- <u>PROOFREAD</u>. The is the final "smoothing out" step. Make certain you proofread your entire document for type-os and grammatical errors. Better still would be to allow someone else to do it that is knowledgeable about your content. While this isn't a deal breaker by any means (quality of content is MUCH more important than quality of grammar), it certainly is a good idea to put your best foot forward.

So, there you have it, the "P.A.G.E.S." system. Each letter stands for one of the five steps in the system...

P - PLAN out your report by brainstorming ideas.
A - ARRANGE your ideas sequentially or systematically.
G - GROW your content by "filling in the blanks".
E - EXTRACT bullet points for your ad copy while you write.
S - SMOOTH out the rough spots to complete the report.

Preparing reports using the P.A.G.E.S. system is just one option. If this looks too tedious, you'll enjoy the next chapter where you'll find a number of shortcuts and less time-consuming approaches for compiling the content for your reports.

7

21 WAYS YOU CAN COMPILE & CREATE AWESOME, HIGHLY DESIRABLE HR INFORMATION …WHILE DOING LITTLE OR NONE OF THE WORK YOURSELF

Many HR folks I talk to are skeptical about putting together a report, even a short one, because it seems entirely too daunting.

In this Chapter, I'm going to show you some ways that you CAN create your own report -- in just a matter of hours -- even if you've never in your life written anything longer than an e-mail.

The secret…

Don't do all the work yourself!

In fact, if you get a little creative, you won't have to do *any* of the work at all! In many of these examples I'm about to share, you don't even have to know a thing about the subject that you'd like to create a product on.

Sound unbelievable.

Here are 21 ways to do it:

YOUR HR GOLDMINE

#1 - USE A GHOSTWRITER

The easiest way to get a report is to just hire *someone else* to write it for you. You can go to a site like elance.com to find a ghostwriter. People release books, reports and articles every day using ghostwriters. They don't have to write a word of it, and they don't even have to be an expert on the subject! It's the easiest way to create a report and start making money quickly!

#2 - INTERVIEW AN EXPERT

If you don't like the ghostwriter idea, that's ok. Another fast and easy way to come up with a high-value, report is to interview an expert on the subject which you want to write about. All this requires is sending an e-mail to one person, who is an authority on the topic of your report, asking him or her to answer a list of predetermined questions. Obviously, the more well-known the expert is, the more marketable your finished product will be. You should create enough questions to fill up a short report (at least 20 pages) after the person answers them.

There are a variety of ways to accomplish this. You could do it by phone, recording the interview and then getting it transcribed into text for your report. Or you could have the conversation via e-mail and then copy and paste it into your report format.

#3 - INTERVIEW SEVERAL EXPERTS

Why utilize one expert when you can tap into several of them? The approach here is similar to #2 above – just with more people. You e-mail a group of people who are authorities in their field, with your request that they answer a short list of specific questions. You then compile all the interviews into one report. You could also have telephone conversations with each of your experts, transcribe them and then copy and paste them all into your report format.

You could pick a general subject, break that up into sub-sections and then interview an expert for each sub-section. For example, if you're creating an report on *Secrets For Filling Hard-to-Fill Engineering Position Quickly,* you could interview an expert on engineering college recruiting, another who is a pro at using social media for recruiting engineers, and another who has experience doing executive search for senior engineering talent, and so on.

#4 - RECORD AND TRANSCRIBE YOUR OWN TIPS AND ADVICE

If you're an expert in a subject yourself, you could get a friend or partner to ask you pre-set questions and record and transcribe those. You can also use a tape recorder and just talk freely into it yourself. Imagine you're talking to a friend and you're giving her advice about X (where "X" is the subject you want to write about.) When you're done, you can type it all out into your computer, or get someone to transcribe it.

You can also get a college student to edit it for you, if you're not comfortable doing your own editing. *Note:* Personally, I prefer to read a report that seems like the author is "talking to me" (it seems more intimate) instead of a report that uses perfect grammar and structure, but ends up being boring.

#5 - RECORD A GROUP CONVERSATION

Invite a small group of people to join in a group conversation with you about a specific topic. Then record it (via Skype or another similar teleconference service), transcribe it, edit the transcripts and turn it into an instant report. Another option is to get everyone together in person at a suitable location – for example, at your home, office, lunch setting, or conference room – then record and transcribe the group conversation.

#6 – CO-AUTHOR A REPORT

Invite writers or experts to co-author a report with you. You could both write it together, and split the workload. The more co-authors you have, the less you'll have to write.

Depending on the number of co-authors you have, you may end up writing only the title and table of contents. The report would be finished in half the time.

The same can be done by involving several experts/authors. Each one would get assigned a portion of the work, say one chapter per author.

#7 - COMPILE EXISTING CONTENT INTO A REPORT

You can just as easily contact a bunch of experts and ask them to submit their best articles on a particular subject. Then, compile them into a report. You could further get instant exposure for your newly created report by giving all the experts who participated the first chance at selling the product to their own customers. (You can also use this strategy with the "interview method" described earlier.)

#8 - BORROW EXISTING CONTENT FROM HR BLOGGERS AND WRITERS

Ask several HR writers to each write a short, original article about a specific subject. Since they are bloggers and writers, and already have existing content, they should be able to provide you with information quickly. Of course, you could offer them incentives to do this. Each expert gets to include their web links at the end of their content so they get free publicity from being included in your report.

The same idea can be used to borrow/reprint sections of reports, audios, or even existing videos. Contact the author and ask for permission to reprint the content in exchange for free publicity.

Here's an example: Let's say you wanted to create a report for "HR leaders." You could contact several writers and bloggers and ask them to provide you with the best blog posts or articles they've ever written on HR leadership. You could compile all the submitted articles into one mega collection of *Success Strategies for HR Leaders.* You got an instant product!

Note: If you decide to utilize this idea, please contact me, I'd be delighted to be included in your report.

#9 - UPDATE OR REPUBLISH EXISTING INFORMATION

Find a special report, e-book, book or manual that's at least a year old and ask the author or publisher for permission to update the information. For example, you could approach the author of the book: *Best Websites for HR Professionals* and offer to help update the information to include all the new resources that came about since the directory was last published – and then republish it as a report. You could also approach the author of an audio CD and ask to convert his product into a report. How about taking a book or e-book on "job search tips" and modifying it into a report for job seekers in the "finance," "sales," or the "information technology" markets.

#10 - PURCHASE "PRIVATE LABEL" RIGHTS

You could search for owners who are already offering private label rights to their written products. As mentioned earlier, private label rights (or PLR) gives you the right to insert 'your name' as the author of the product, take credit for it, and sell it for any price you choose even though you did not write it. You own it. And as the owner of the PLR, you can do anything with it you choose: you can change the graphics, you can change the content and you can "customize" it to fit your audience.

To find PLR reports, articles and reports, just google the words "PLR," "PLR eBooks," "private label rights" or "resale rights" and you will be amazed at the content that you can buy and own at very reasonable prices.

#11 – GO BACK THROUGH YOUR OLD HR FILES AND ARCHIVES

If you're a packrat like I am, chances are you have lots of old reports, memos, PowerPoint presentations, training programs and papers you've created over the years. Dig them out. This may mean going back through all your past HR jobs and all the files you've kept. Of course, you'll want to wipe out any confidential or proprietary information related to any of your past employers, but you may find that you've already written enough to create your report.

#12 - COMPILE EXCERPTS FROM LINKEDIN DISCUSSION GROUPS

LinkedIn groups are a wealth of information. Lots of expert advice is disseminated through these groups daily through group discussions and Q&A. If you come across a topic in one of the groups you want to expand into a report, send an e-mail to the participants, asking their permission to use either an excerpt of a posting or the full postings on a certain topic.

#13 - USE PUBLIC DOMAIN INFORMATION

Using Public Domain information is an easy way to compile a report quickly. Why? Because there is so much of it. There are literally millions upon millions of public domain works available that you can use. Most people don't know what public domain is, so let me explain. It's information whose copyright has expired or information that never had a copyright in the first place. For example, all of the William Shakespeare plays are copyright-free information because there were never copyrights placed on them. The original *King James Bible* is also copyright free information.

YOUR HR GOLDMINE

So how do you get at all this public domain content? There are two sources I recommend:

- *Government Public Domain.* When the U.S. government creates or commissions information, it is paid for by federal taxes and therefore owned by the taxpayers. Almost all the time, U.S. government information is in the public domain and not copyrighted. (Documents that are exceptions to this rule carry a copyright notice.) This means that anyone has the right to republish that information however they please, as if they had researched and created it themselves. You have the right to publish it exactly as is, change the format, chop it into smaller pieces, rewrite it, combine it with other public domain or proprietary information or translate it - all without charge and without needing to request permission. The best resource for government public domain information is *FirstGov.gov.* This is a search engine specifically for the government that they put together for us. Many of the publications on that site will have PDFs already done for you. You can take and rewrite them and start marketing them immediately.
- *Project Gutenberg.* Most people have heard of Project Gutenberg. If you go to Gutenberg.org, they have over 20,000 free public domain reports. They are free because their copyright has already expired. Even better: these books are already in digital format in their catalog and can be easily downloaded.

With all this free content at your fingertips, you could easily create your first product by republishing, re-authoring, re-titling and/or repackaging the public domain information.

One final point: If information is available free online, why would people pay for it? Here's why. Many folks don't have the time or skills to find free information online. If you can bring information of interest to them to their attention, they may be as willing to pay for it as they do for other books, recordings, etc. This is especially true if you package the material clearly, attractively, conveniently and understandably.

#14 – USE CASE STUDIES

Ask several experts to offer a case study of their most recent project. For example, if you're writing about *performance appraisal approaches,* you would ask each contributor to give you a brief write copy of their last 'successful' performance appraisal form and process; and explain the what/why/how of the reason for its success. Compile these case study examples into a guide that you can sell.

#15 - CHECKLISTS AND/OR "TOP 10" LISTS

Create (or ask an expert to put together) a simple checklist that one could use as to guide them through a difficult process. For example, you could put together a detailed 'checklist' which would guide someone through preparing for a labor negotiation. It would ensure that they have thought through all the considerations prior to their first meeting with their union counterpart. You could also use the same idea to create a "Top 10…" list for any subject. Example: *"Top 10 Ways To Improve Your Preparation & Success in Conducting Labor Negotiations."*

#16 - SELL YOUR IDEAS

Instead of creating the products yourself, you could put together a 20-40 page report that lists all of your creative ideas, so that others could use them to create their own products (kind of like what I'm doing with this list).

#17 - HOLD A CONTEST

Example: If you'd like to write a report on "low-cost, creative ways to recognize high-performing employees" you could hold a contest and ask everyone to submit their best ideas/designs and allow you reprint rights to the submissions. Then, compile all the submissions into one report.

#18 - TEMPLATES OR TOOLS

Compile into a report a collection of templates, tools, or models. For example, you could ask for sample job descriptions for certain "benchmark" positions that other people could use as templates or models in writing their own job descriptions. Other ideas you could consider include compiling sample resumes, termination letters, employment contracts, assessment tools, disciplinary or reprimand letters, or employee survey questions. Any one of these ideas would make a great report that could be created quickly.

#19 - RESOURCES LIST

You could very easily compile list of useful resources on certain subjects and turn that into a product. For example: a list of free personal development webinars, free employee survey software, e-learning courses, etc.

#20 - DIRECTORIES AND GUIDES

Pick a target group and create a directory and guide just for them. Example: You could also create a directory of the best HR websites for Organization Development professionals (or any other specialized group). This could include a list of the best online sources for managing their careers, finding a job, becoming a consultant, and/or tools they can use with their clients.

#21 - CAPITALIZE ON TRENDS AND FADS

Piggybacking on trends and fads is an easy way to create a bestseller. Years ago, when the *Reengineering the Corporation* book hit corporate America, and companies of all sizes started to "re-engineer" their companies, people started selling anything and everything that even remotely tied to reengineering in some way. And, HR folks, operating managers, leaders, executives, even employees bought 'em all! Nobody wanted to be caught flat-footed not knowing what that craze was all about. It didn't matter that most people totally misunderstood what it was truly all about (business process improvement, not headcount reductions). People were hungry for information! The same thing is happening now with trends such as "employee engagement" and "social media." Question for you: What current hot trend or fad could you attach to YOUR report?

So, there you have it, 21 ways you can create your own report quickly...in many cases, in just a matter of hours...while doing little or none of the work yourself.

8

STEP FOUR: HOW TO PACKAGE, PRICE AND POSITION YOUR HR KNOW-HOW & INFORMATION FOR MEGA-SUCCESS

Now that you've gathered the actual content for your short report – either by writing it yourself or by using one of the "little or no writing" techniques -- you'll want to get it ready to sell by putting on a few finishing touches.

These final touches involve packaging, pricing, and positioning it for sale.

PART 1:
PACKAGING YOUR REPORT

When it comes to "packaging" your report, there are two basic things you want to address: the "contents" and the "cosmetics".

Contents

In addition to the information in your report, you need other "pages" to complete its construction. In order of appearance within your finished report, they are…

1: Title page. This typically will include the title of your report, any subtitle, your name as author and possibly your website address, contact information and any graphics you might want to include.

2: Legal page. This necessary page of your report would include copyright information, disclaimers, terms of usage and any extra special disclosures or instructions you might have. There's a "Disclaimer & Legal Notice" included on the copyright page in the front of this book that you can refer to in crafting one for your report.

3: Author page. You should always include a page about yourself in your short report for a couple of solid reasons: it allows your readers to identify with you. It also brands you and allows you to inform the reader of other resources you may offer such as other reports, consulting, book or advice. Finally, it helps you to build relationships by allowing them to link to your social media sites (LinkedIn, Twitter, Facebook, Google+, your blog, etc).

4: Table of contents. (Optional) This is the one page of your report that is optional. Typically, if your report is 20 pages or less, you really don't need a table of contents. Only use a table of contents if your report is 30 to 40 pages and has distinct chapter separations that are worth noting in advance.

5: Report. Next comes the report itself. As we've talked about repeatedly, this would be at least 20 pages in length, with a maximum of 40 pages. After your featured information, there is one final element to the "contents" of your short report…and it is…

6: Backend page. There should always be some kind of "backend" offer at the end of your report. This can be something as blatant as a full-blown advertisement for a high-ticket product or something as subtle as a brief listing of your consulting services or other reports you have available for purchase.

> **Your <u>Minimum</u> Backend Page:
> "Recommended Resources"**
>
> What I consider to be a minimum backend page is a list of at least 3-4 *"recommend resources"* that are related to the content of your short report. These can either be your own related offers or those you are promoting as a paid affiliate for another author. For example: If your report is titled: *"Ten Keys To Success as an Internal Organization Development Consultant,"* you might list these (made up) additional "recommended resources" at the conclusion of your report that are offered by other authors...
>
> - *Time Management for Internal Organization Development Consultants*
> - *The Beginner's Guide to Internal Organization Consulting*
> - *10 Quick Team Building Exercises for Internal Organization Consultants*
>
> **Hint**: Look for recommended resources by authors who have a "freebie" available at their main sales page, such as a free report, newsletter or tutorials. This will allow you to offer this freebie to your audience...thereby providing a service to your customers, generating more interest, and ultimately getting more readers to buy the actual product itself...which will earn you backend profits through your commission on the sale.

So, those are the highlights of packaging your report as far as the "contents" are concerned. Now let's talk about...

Cosmetics

As we've discussed, "Contents" cover WHAT to include in your report. By contrast, the "Cosmetics" focus on HOW you should include those things. In other words, how does your report LOOK? Appearance is crucial.

YOUR HR GOLDMINE

There's a big difference between something scribbled in crayons and something etched in calligraphy. While we aren't striving for a work of art here, it is our aim to create something aesthetically pleasing, not an eyesore.

So, here are 8 things you'll want to do in order to sharpen the appearance of your report.

1: Header and Footer. The layout of your content pages begins with a "header" and "footer". These appear on every page of your report, with the exception of your title page (page one). To be crystal clear (and yes, maybe I'm being just a little anal) the "header" appears at the very top of the page and the "footer" appears at the bottom of the page. Got it. Ok.

For the header: I recommend putting the title of the report in bold in the header, with a horizontal line beneath it to separate it from the remainder of the page.

For the footer: I would suggest putting your name and website or your e-mail address in the footer. Additionally, it doesn't hurt to put a horizontal line above the text to separate it from the remainder of the page.

2: Margins. I have observed some marked differences in the size of margins in the many years I've been reading other people's reports. Some blatantly use 1.5"-2.0" margins in an attempt to produce "more pages" with the same amount of text. These same folks use 20 point text for the same purpose. Resist the temptation to join them. You don't need to attempt any sleight of hand tactics – which are quite obvious, by the way – to "pad" your length. It's not quantity we're after in reports, it's quality. *The point is to be to the point!* I recommend .75" margins with additional space at the top and bottom for your header and footer.

3: Fonts. There are a lot of well-used fonts that you can choose from in creating your report. Some of the most popular are Times New Roman, Helvetica, Arial, Courier, Tahoma and Verdana. Personally, I don't have a preferred font. Any of these

I've mentioned work well. What I don't recommend is trying to get cute by using some of the fancier fonts. While they may look nice at first, many other fonts become difficult to read after a period of time and could detract from your work.

It's also a good idea to stick with standard 12 point text size. In the words of Goldilocks, *"this one's just right"*.

4: Headlines. When you arrive at new chapters, distinctions, listings or any other kind of "separation / divider" in your report, re-focus your reader's attention by using boldface, larger text headlines. I generally use 18 point Tahoma in bold style. This serves a dual purpose: (1) to separate key sections and thoughts from the remainder of the text, and (2) to add another design element to the appearance of the text.

5: Indentions and Boxes. Indentions and boxes are two more nice "cosmetics" you can use to improve the flow of reading and add another dimension to your report's layout. I recommend that you use indentions and boxes to separate key thoughts, create bullet lists, define words and expressions, provide case studies, to give a closer look, make a recommendation or offer an example.

6: Styles. One of the most commonly used design elements of your report could be font "styles" such as *italics*, **bold** and <u>underline</u>. These are especially useful in creating distinctions and placing emphasis on important points or inflections. Please note that the **numbering** <u>and</u> *type of cosmetic* in this list of styles is highlighted in a font style. And, please further note that I just drew your attention to the words "numbering", "and" and "type of cosmetic" in the previous sentence by using font styles. This is very effective in streamlining your content and getting your point across in important spots.

7: Graphics | Screenshots | Photographs. There will be times when you'll want to use graphics, screenshots and photographs in your report. I have a simple rule of thumb when it comes to

using these elements: use them ONLY when they are helpful or needed.
- If you're writing a tutorial for using a software program, then screenshots of the application's interface would be helpful, thus a good idea.
- If you're writing a report on organizing your office and want to include "before-and-after" photographs of a messy versus a well-organized office, then that's also a good idea.
- However, if you want to insert some animated graphic of a clock because you happened to mention a clock in the paragraph, that's not necessarily the best use of your space.

8: Use a PDF format for your report. There's one final thing I need to address about "packaging." There are a LOT of report compiler software programs available on the Internet that you can use in order to create your actual "downloadable, digital version" of the report to sell online. I recommend that you deliver your report in a PDF format for three simple reasons:
- *It's universal.* Both PC and Mac users can access PDFs just fine. MAC users have problems accessing some .exe reports created with a lot of the "e-book compiler" programs on the market.
- *It's user-friendly.* You don't need to create complicated HTML pages. You don't need to create complex special links to go from page to page. You don't need to create navigational menus. You just convert your Word document directly into PDF. It's simple.
- *It's un-problematic.* I've very rarely heard of anyone having trouble viewing a PDF file. I've heard a gazillion stories from people having trouble viewing reports, white papers and e-books created with other tools. PDF has become the standard of digital information delivery in compiled form for good reason: it works.

Adobe Acrobat Professional is great for converting PDFs with the click of one button. However, it can be a bit pricey. If budget is an issue, then I have two recommendations for you:

First, check eBay for earlier versions of the software. These previous releases will get the job done just fine and can often be found at a fraction of the cost of the latest release.

Secondly, you can find quite a few alternatives to Adobe Acrobat online – some even for free – by doing a Google search for "PDF maker" or "convert to PDF" or "PDF software."

Okay, having taken a lengthy look at "packaging", let's spend some time talking about "pricing"…

PART 2:
PRICING YOUR REPORT

Over and over again, the same question comes up in regards to selling your report: *how much should I charge for it?*

There are all kinds of formulas for determining price that we won't go into because most are more confusing than they are useful. Let me sum up three simple "rules" that, to me, govern the amount you should charge for your reports.

Rule #1: Your <u>content</u> is the most important factor in determining your price. You can pretty much answer "how much should I charge for it" by answering "how much is it worth?"

Think about it: How much would YOU pay for a 20 page report. Well, that depends, of course, on what the report is about. If it's 20 pages of "how to mud-wrestle an angry crocodile," then chances are you wouldn't pay much for the report. On the other hand, if the 20 pages contained a description of 20 employers in your city who are ready to hire you and increase your salary by 25% right now, the information would be quite valuable to you and the amount you'd spend for it would bear this out.

Let's look at this another way. If your name is John Smith and you demand a $20 million a year contract with the Chicago Bulls pro basketball team, you're going to be out of luck because you can't deliver the goods. However, if your name happens to be Michael Jordan or Derrick Rose and you can demand that contract, you WILL probably get it because you CAN bring that kind of value to the table.

The point is this: How much you charge for your report depends on how much value it delivers and how good it is. That's the most important factor in determining its price. Can it deliver the goods?

Rule #2: Your <u>competition's</u> inadequacies help place a premium on your content. Listen, if you've got something that works which others don't have, that's going have a big impact upon the price (and demand!) of your report. Few people will buy a report on something of interest to them if it's the same old thing they've already read a thousand times before. But, if you can prove that you know some *secret*, have some *special insight*, possess some *short cut*, can point to some *advantage* that your competition doesn't have, then your report's "value" just went up a few more notches.

What's missing from what your competition is offering that you have in your report? Focus on that and you'll find customers focused on you!

Rule #3: Your <u>customer's</u> expectations, buying habits and desires make the final decision. Ultimately, the right price is in the hands of your potential customers. They make the final decision as to whether or not they are willing to pay X price for your short report.

There are several different factors that influence their buying decisions including:
- What they reasonably expect to receive from your report.
- What they are accustomed to paying for similar offers.
- How much of a desire they have for your report at this time.

The good news is: you can, to some degree, have influence over all of this.

YOUR HR GOLDMINE

Now, having given you some rules for pricing, let me provide you with a VERY general "guideline" when it comes to pricing your short report...which is to price your reports at around $0.75-$1.00 per page.

Length of Report	Your Price
20-25 pages	$10 - $20
25-30 pages	$20 - $30
30-40 pages*	$25 - $40

*Anything more than 40 pages is no longer a short report, it's a manual or short book.

Again, if your report contains hard-to-find, expert information with a much higher value, then your pricing would be different.

But, for most reports, this is a good guideline to price by. Unless you have some significant reason to look at a different pricing structure, stick with this one.

Okay, we now want to talk about "Part 3: Positioning"...

BUT FIRST, A CAUTION: If you're a beginner or relatively new to selling your HR knowledge, you might want to just skip the rest of this chapter and don't worry about it right now. What we're about to talk about is optional. It's a way to gain an edge, but if it's over your head, it's not important for you right now. It's not critical. It's just something I do need to discuss in order to be complete and help users at all levels of experience. Now with that said, let's now move on to...

PART 3:
POSITIONING YOUR REPORT

Now, without delving too deep into positioning – which could be a rather lengthy discussion in itself – what I want to help you do is to develop what marketing people call a "USP" or "unique sales proposition."

> **Defined: Your "Unique Sales Position"**
> An intentional, clearly visible means of separating yourself from others to create a competitive edge. It's what makes you *different* from others that you use as an advantage. It's what about you that's better than the rest stated in a way that engages your target audience. That's your "unique sales proposition".

Let me tell you a story to more clearly illustrate this point...

Bill is a good friend of mine from my days in HR at PepsiCo. And, like me, admits he could stand to lose a few pounds. When he married his lovely wife 12 years ago, he had a 28 inch waist and weighed in at a whopping 155 pounds. He worked out 5 days a week and was on top of his game.

Something happened during the past 12 years. He developed a new hobby called eating.

Recently, he decided it was time to tone up again. His goal is simple: to get back into the best physical shape of his life. At age 36, it's not going to be as easy as it was back at 24, but then again, he has always been up for a good challenge.

So, today he went out looking at equipment. While shopping, he happened to spot a shelf of exercise balls. You know, the big bright blue balls that you inflate and do various exercises on. Having seen that they can be useful in toning abdominal muscles (which is where he wants to start), he decided to take a closer look.

Here's what he discovered that all these products had in common...

Four completely identical bright blue exercise balls.

We're talking the exact same size.

The exact same yellow foot pump to inflate the ball.

YOUR HR GOLDMINE

The exact same tube of glue to repair the ball should you decide to take a razor blade and slice it to bits after a few days of frustration. (Hey, just kidding).

Anyway, three of the products sold for the exact same price of $12.99. The fourth product had an asking price of $16.99.

He immediately decided he would buy the $16.99 version.

Why spend more money for the exact same product?

Here's why...

Product A, B and C all had the standard product name of *Brand A Exercise Ball*, *Brand B Exercise Ball* and *Brand C Exercise Ball*. They all showed basically the same photographs of various exercises and the benefits were all basically the same.

Product D was entitled -- get this -- *Awesome Abs Exercise Ball*. And the exercises it showed were all designed to strengthen and tone abdominal muscles.

Listen closely because this is the key...

It was the EXACT same product as the others, but had a different focus!

So he bought it.

Ok, but what does that have to do with you?

In a word: Everything.

Here are the three big lessons to learn here...

Lesson #1: "**You can sell the same product at a higher price than your competition.**" Forget about this nonsense that says you should undercut your competitor in price to be successful. Not true. Lower price doesn't mean greater sales. To the contrary, you can actually RAISE YOUR PRICE and sell more than ever. And here's how...

Lesson #2: "**The key to selling at a higher price is POSITIONING.**" It's all about how you PRESENT your offer.

It's all about how you PACKAGE your offer. It's about your POSITION. A quarter pound hamburger might cost you $2-$3 at McDonald's. They are "budget fast food." The same quarter pound hamburger will cost you around $9.95 at Red Robin. They bill themselves as offering "gourmet hamburgers." What's the difference? Their position within the industry.

Lesson #3: **"An easy way to position yourself for profits is to focus on a niche."** Jack Trout, the leading expert on positioning, teaches two things about positioning (actually, MANY things, but we'll narrow it down to two for now)... (1) It's better to be first in your people's mind than better and (2) If you can't be first in their minds in one category create a new category.

That's what the *Awesome Abs Exercise Ball* did. It probably wasn't the first exercise ball on the market. But, it's the only exercise ball I've ever seen to date that is focused on *abdominal muscles*. It has positioned itself to focus on a NICHE market where it can be FIRST.

So, the bottom line is this...

You can SELL MORE if you POSITION yourself FIRST in a SPECIFIC NICHE market.

Now, what does all of that mean for you and your report? Let's get personal here and talk about creating YOUR "unique sales position."

While there are many different aspects of developing a USP, I want to look at the two easiest things you can do to develop your own presence and really separate yourself from your competition in an advantageous way. (Let's call these Lessons #3A & #3B).

Lesson #3A: One way you can separate yourself from your competition by focusing on a specific BENEFIT. What is it that you've got which no one else does? Specifically, what about your report makes it special? What's different? What's exclusive?

- Is it the only report available on the topic?
- Does it have more ideas than any other report?
- Have you broken things down into the easiest-to-follow steps?
- Does it include something that's missing from others?
- Is it written in a more "user-friendly" language?
- Does it include helpful screenshots?
- Do you reveal some little known fact or secret strategy?
- Have you produced some staggering results?
- Is it a completely different approach to the subject?
- Does it contain the latest information or updated ideas?
- Does it disclose something that's "top secret"?
- Is it the most complete report available?
- Does it explain things in greater detail?
- Is it full of ways to apply existing information?
- Does it have brainstorming exercises?
- Does it include things like forms and worksheets?
- Is it specifically for "advanced users"?
- Does it expand upon an existing concept?
- Does it offer an easier or faster way to accomplish a task?
- Does it offer a different solution to a common problem?

I've just given you 20 different ways that your report can be "positioned" in a unique way. Surely there is something on this list 20 questions that you can respond to with an emphatic "yes!"

Listen, you've got something in that report that no one else has and that's what we need to determine. What is it about your report that makes it stand out among what others are offering?

Key in on that. This is going to be especially important in just a few minutes as we begin talking about the sales message for your report. Focus on a specific "benefit" to the reader – what can you offer them that no one else can?

Now let's go on to...

Lesson #3B: The other way to separate yourself from your competition is to focus on a specific <u>CROWD</u>. That is, position your report for a specific target group. With this approach, the focus is less on WHAT you're teaching in the report and more on WHO you're teaching it to.

(By the way, this is my book, and if you've read any of my stuff you'll know that I dangle my participles and use fragmented sentences. ☺ This is a perfect time for me to mention that – unless your report is about grammar - most people don't care if you don't know your punctuation from your preposition. It's all about your content. It doesn't have to impress your high school English teacher. If your customers had wanted an eloquent work, they'd have ordered a poetry book instead of your report. And if you're one of those people who can't get past the fact that I put a comma in the wrong place or used the word "there" when it should have been "their," I would say to you ... this isn't a homework assignment, so stop trying to grade it and focus on why you bought it in the first place – to LEARN SOMETHING. ☺)

Anyway, I digress. Back to the point: You can also focus on a specific *crowd* in order to position your report. That's another aspect of what the *Awesome Abs Ball* folks did. They focused on a specific group of people: those wanting to tone up their abs.

You can do this too, in a couple of specific ways...

By Experience or Skill Level. Focus your report on the experience level of other people. In other words, your report is specifically for *"beginners"* or those who are *"experienced"* or people in between. Here are a few examples.

- Example 1: If you're writing a report about "getting HR certification," it can be specifically targeted for "those who didn't pass the certification exam the first time." In this example, that's what makes you different. While others might offer resources for EVERYONE interested in attaining certification, yours is exclusively for those who have made an unsuccessful attempt.
- Example 2: If you're writing a report about "facilitating groups," you could focus it on those who are experienced facilitators. Since I've facilitated lots of

groups in my HR career, I'd be much more likely to buy something related to my skill level than a report for beginners.

- Example 3: If you're writing a report about "negotiating union contracts," then you might position it specifically for "the first-time negotiator." Again, that makes you different.
- Example 4: If you're writing a report about "using social media to land a job," you might want to focus it on different levels of experience such as: for beginners who are not social media savvy, for those who already have a LinkedIn or Facebook presence, for those who are already making $150K a year, etc.

So, that's one way of distinguishing yourself by targeting specific groups based on "experience and skill levels."

By Distinction. In this strategy, you focus on some "adjective" that describes a group of people. Again, here are some classic examples:

- Example 1: If you're writing a report about "change management," then you could target it towards "consultants," "line managers," or "academics" with specific examples drawn from your own experience.
- Example 2: If you're writing a report about "strategies for getting promoted," you could focus it on "engineers," "accountants," "marketers," or any other distinctive group of people who are interested in advancing their career.
- Example 3: If you're writing a report about "improving diversity in the workplace" you could focus it specifically on "women," "Latinos," "LGBTs," or the "disabled." And, to take the point further, you could be even more selective by targeting the "Latino disabled," or "gay women."

Again, the idea here is find a distinctive group of people and target them with your report. While most of your competition is catering to the masses, you've separated yourself by going after a slightly smaller demographic among the general audience.

That's how you can position your report in order to make it more desirable to your potential customers and create an advantage over your competition.

All you need to do is to answer just two questions:

(1) What does my report offer that no one else does?

(2) Who would my report be just perfect for?

Obviously, the **best option** would be to position your report in both ways: by focusing on a specific benefit <u>AND</u> a specific group, which is what the *Awesome Abs* folks did.

☆ BONUS SHORTCUT!
THERE'S NO NEED TO READ CHAPTERS 9 & 10
IF YOU DECIDE TO DO THE FOLLOWING...

The next two chapters will show you how to create your own website and sales message to sell your report. This was the only *online* option until a few years ago. Now there's another way.

You can sell your special reports at the **Amazon Kindle Store.** By doing this, you will bypass a lot of the work described in Chapters 9 & 10 because you won't need to create a website, sales message or find an order processor.

Why? Because Amazon will provide all these services for you...FREE. You can have your own unique webpage just like the thousands of other Kindle e-book sellers have...plus Amazon will deliver your reports AND collect payments for you. All you do is refer customers to your Amazon site to buy your 20-40 page report (now called an "e-book") which they can then download to their Kindles, iPads, smartphones, and other e-readers.

If you like this option, go back and re-read pages 36-38 and follow the instructions there and your Kindle report/e-book will appear on Amazon in just a few days.

The downside to all this is that Amazon Kindle's commission structure of 35-70% will deliver a lot less profit to you than the other methods in Chapters 9 & 10, which are my first choices. Nevertheless, Amazon is a solid option.

9

STEP FIVE:
PUTTING TOGETHER A POWERFUL SALES MESSAGE THAT CREATES HUGE DEMAND FOR YOUR HR EXPERTISE, ADVICE & KNOW-HOW

Once you finish preparing your report to sell online, it's time to shift your focus to the actual sales process. And that process is going to begin with your "one page sales message." It's a one page sales message because it takes up about one page on the website that you will use to sell your report.

    Everyone has their own way of developing a sales message, but the basic components are the same. And it is these basic components that I'm going to cover for you in this chapter.

IMPORTANT SIDEBAR:
Creating The One-Page Website For Your Sales Message

Before we begin looking at the process of crafting a sales message for your report, I need to mention that you'll need some kind of software program in order to put your message on a webpage so that it can be viewed online. You have two options:

1. **If you've NOT created web pages before...**the fastest way to get this done is to hire someone to create a sales page for you and upload it to your domain name. This is a relatively simple and inexpensive programming task. You probably know a teenager who can handle it for $20 and a pizza. If not, there are plenty of web designers you can hire at Elance.com for $25 to $30 who can do this for you in a couple of hours. All you have to do is go to the Elance.com site and post a description of what you want done...which is to create a one page site with your sales message with 4 other items (e.g. an order button, your report, graphics plus a download page – all of which I'll cover in Chapter 10). But let me not get ahead of myself. For now, just have peace of mind that you can outsource all of the web page development quickly, easily and cheaply...if you're not a techie.

2. **If you HAVE created web pages before or want to create your own sales message page...**there are a number of simple sales page templates you can use. OptimizePress is a sales page template that works on the WordPress platform and is highly recommended. Or if you want to explore even more options than just this one, just google "sales page templates."

Just in case you're curious, I use Microsoft FrontPage and have been using it for years. It's kind of old school (I use the 2003 version) but it works – and it does an excellent, excellent job of creating sales pages! I've used it for all my special reports and books. It does take time to learn, but I highly recommend it.

Having said all of that, let's begin looking at the process of writing a one page sales message that you will provide on a website in order to get visitors to buy your report.

As we make our way through the 11 basic parts of your sales message, I'll be using as an example one of my most successful sales messages.

It's the one that has been used to sell hundreds of copies of my 61-page report, *Start Your Own Awesome HR Blog* (pictured on the left) which you can find at AwesomeHRBlog.com.

Note: Even though this report is a few pages longer than the 20-40 pages that I recommend, the same principles and concepts apply.

11 PARTS OF AN ORDER-PRODUCING ONE PAGE SALES MESSAGE FOR YOUR REPORT

PART 1: THE PRE-HEAD

The first part of your sales message is what's known as the "pre-head." This is a short, introductory statement located at the very top of your sales page that is used to…
- Engage the reader's attention.
- Quickly introduce a key idea or qualification.
- Set the stage for the thrust of the sales message.

There isn't a set in stone rule for the length of a pre-headline. I've seen a prehead consisting of only one word – and I've seen a complete paragraph. Generally speaking, use as few words as possible to effectively communicate your message.

Here are some examples…

(Mention A Specific Group)
"Attention First-Time Managers..."

(Mention A Specific Problem With Latest Development)
"New Breakthrough Discovery For Reducing EEO Lawsuits…"

YOUR HR GOLDMINE

(Mention A Credible Source)
"As Featured At the National SHRM Conference..."

(Mention A Shocking Announcement)
"You've Been Lied To About How To Get Promoted in HR"

(Mention A Statement Of Fact)
"A Panel Of Top Leadership Experts Agree, This Is The Easiest Way To..."

In my report, *Start Your Own Awesome HR Blog,* I used the following as my pre-head...

Attention: HR Professionals, Leaders & Consultants!
Are you frustrated with the progress you've made in your HR career? Would you like to differentiate yourself from the rest of the pack in HR?

This begins the sales message and provides a number of other benefits for the reader.

It targets the group that this sales message is for (HR professionals, leaders and consultants).

It gets their attention – "Are you frustrated with the progress you've made in your HR career?"

It introduces a key idea that I'll be expanding on later in the sales message – "how to differentiate yourself from the rest of the pack in HR."

And, you'll find out next, it seamlessly launches into the primary headline.

Speaking of which, that's the second part of your sales message that we want to direct our attention to next...

PART 2: THE PRIMARY HEAD

This is your main headline – located at the top center of your sales page immediately below your pre-head. It should be in

larger, bolder print and may contain certain words highlighted in different colored text for emphasis.

As an example, in my *Start Your Own Awesome HR Blog* sales message, the main headline is…

"Take Your Human Resources Career To The Next Level By Launching YOUR OWN HR Blog!"
Discover Secrets for Starting Up Your Own Outrageously Successful Human Resources Blog… Even If You're An Absolute Beginner…Step-by-Step, Quickly & From Scratch!

The primary head of your report is your biggest weapon of the sales page and should be used to showcase your biggest benefit to the reader. It should answer the following questions:

- What is the ultimate "best reason" someone should buy your report?
- What is the most desirable result of buying your report to the reader?
- What, above everything else, would be most beneficial about buying it?

This is your chance to quickly encapsulate your entire sales message in 1-2 eye-catching sentences that are GUARANTEED to be read by <u>every</u> <u>single</u> <u>visitor</u> to your site.

Fire your biggest gun!

Now there are a lot of different models, templates and "*kinds*" of headlines that have been repeatedly used over the years which have proven to be very effective in producing orders.

I can't possibly cover them all, but let me share with you one that has really **generated great results** for many people – and their clients.

It's called the "*If You Can, Then You Can*" model.

The idea is to make a simple, reasonable qualification that the reader must meet (that's the *"If You Can"* part) in order to reap some tremendous result (that's the *"Then You Can"* part) of great interest to them.

Here's an example:

"If You Can Write <u>20-40 Page Tiny, Little Reports</u>, Then You Can Create A Great Source of Extra Income For Yourself In Just <u>A Few Hours</u> Each Week…Working From The Comfort Of Your Home And Without Leaving Your HR Day Job!"

As with any type of ad or sales copy, there are some key points to remember in creating your headline…

Use Particulars. The more specific you can be, the better. Not only will your statements seem more believable with specifics, but in many instances they can seem more reachable. It's not just "write reports," it's "write 10-40 page reports."

Use Periods. One of the things most people want is a "time frame." How long will this take? When can I expect results? It's not just "creating a great source of extra income for yourself," it's "create a great source of extra income for yourself in JUST A FEW HOURS each week…"

Use Pictures. Unless they're a glutton for punishment, most people want the easiest route to their destination of choice…and without taking big risks. Use word pictures to describe the ultimate result most desirable to the reader. It's not just "working from home," it's "working from the comfort of your home and without leaving your current HR day job."

So, there's a lot to convey in your headline. It sets the tone for your entire sales message, so spend some time developing it based on the things we've talked about here. By simply making some appropriate substitutions into the *"If You Can, Then You Can"* headline model, you should be able to craft an attention-grabbing start to your one page sales message.

PART 3: THE POST-HEAD

This is similar to the "pre-head" in that it's a brief connecting statement. This time, it bridges the gap from the headline to the opening paragraph of your copy.

Now, again, for you there are a lot of different ideas you can use for your post-head.

Make A Statement Of Emphasis. In other words, briefly expand upon what you said in the headline – but emphasize something that will make it even EASIER or FASTER or MORE REWARDING than what you've already stated. I used this technique in my *Start Your Own Awesome HR Blog* report. The post-head is...

Showcase your expertise, gain instant credibility & boost your HR career!

Notice the emphasis on the "end result" that the reader could be expected to achieve by purchasing my report. The point is the post-head is used to place emphasis on an easier, faster or more rewarding aspect of what I'm about to share in my message to the reader.

Mention A Deadline Or Limit. Another good use of your post-head is to begin creating urgency by stressing some kind of deadline or limit that you are imposing. A few examples include...

"80% Off Introductory Price Ends On October 12th at Midnight!" There Are Just ~~24~~ 16 Copies Left Before We'll Be Sold Out!"

Obviously, you'll need to give more details on this deadline later towards the end of your sales message, but this is a great place to introduce a legitimate deadline to your reader.

Now, once you have a post-head in place, you're ready to go into the main body of your sales message, starting with your first paragraph which includes...

PART 4: THE PROBLEM.

Virtually every good sales message begins in one form or another with an introduction of a problem. Some examples:

YOUR HR GOLDMINE

- You're not getting enough recognition on the job.
- Your salary isn't high enough.
- You don't know where to start in developing a strategic plan.
- You need to figure out a way to cut costs.
- You can't seem to manage your time.
- You're not as good at leading others as you'd like to be.
- You're really interested in leveraging social media.
- You could be happier if just one thing changed.

Serious or trivial, stated positively or negatively, real or imagined, problems are the universal driving force behind many – if not most - decisions we make. We want to avoid them, correct them, minimize them or make up for them, but make no mistake about it, they have great influence in our lives.

We'd be happier without problems, or so we think. We'd at least try to give it a try. ☺ And, if we can't completely eliminate our problems, it sure would be nice to have something really wonderful happening in our lives that would diminish or overshadow them. We all have things that we'd like to improve upon. Things we'd like to see changed to some degree. Things we'd like to make better.

So, one of the best ways you can begin your one page sales message is to establish the fact that there is a *problem* that needs to be addressed. Generally, by telling some kind of story that allows you to identify with the reader and the problem they face.

Here's an example of part of an opening for the sales message for **Start Your Own Awesome HR Blog…**

> *Are you frustrated with the progress you've made in your HR career? Would you like to differentiate yourself from the rest of the pack in HR? If so, then having your own HR blog is an <u>absolute</u> <u>must.</u>*
>
> *Your own blog allows you to showcase your expertise, gain instant credibility and enhance your HR career.*
>
> *It doesn't matter where you are in your HR career right now. You can be a newbie just getting started in your first HR job. Or a 10-year HR veteran. Or an ex-*

perienced specialist in compensation, labor relations, staffing or OD. Or an independent consultant, coach or contract professional. Or a vice president of HR. It just doesn't matter.

Blogging can brand you and set you apart from the rest of the HR pack. And, the exposure you get from your blog allows you to be easily contacted by clients, potential employers, hiring managers, headhunters, and others who can help advance your HR career.

See how the problem was presented here? See how we empathized with the reader? And see how we then hinted at the ability to make a positive change for her? It's an easy transition from here to the next "part" of the sales message, which is...

PART 5: PRODUCT

Now that you've established a problem, it's time to share the solution – namely, your report and what it offers.

First of all, let's talk about your report itself.

Here's a cardinal rule to pay very close attention to: When you hear that people don't judge a book by the cover, that's a lie.

People do.

Even reports. It's human nature. It's the same as when you meet a person for the first time, no matter how unbiased you feel you are, you judge them based on how they appear before you -- long before they open their mouths and express themselves.

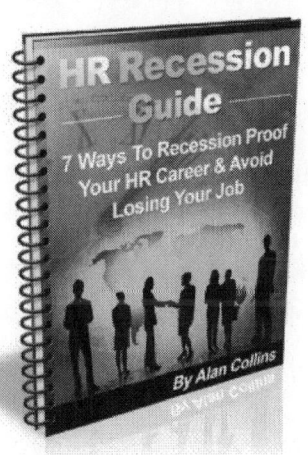

Image is key to your report's success because when people first see it online, it must "look" attractive and desirable. So, no matter what your report is about, similar to the example to the left, it is crucial that you have an **im-**

age of your report on your sales page if you want to boost the positive first impressions about your report, its credibility and increase your sales.

I recommend that you don't create the cover yourself, especially if you're inexperienced in Photoshop or graphics. There are some great report cover graphic designers around on the cheap. A simple search on Google will uncover many them that will charge between $20 -$90 to do a cover for your report for you. If you're on a budget, you'll be able to find some awesome ecover designers on **fiverr.com**. You can have a professionally-done report cover done there for $5 and have it delivered to you in 1-2 days. That's right - $5. All you have to do is sign-up for their service (free) and do a search for "ebook covers" and you'll find lots of designers who will deliver a professional looking cover ideal for your special report for five bucks. If your report is between 20-40 pages, I do recommend using the spiral bound type e-cover (like the one pictured) to convey that this is a short report not, a book.

So that's the skinny on report covers.

Let's now talk about the second part of presenting your product in your sales message, which is what YOU are specifically offering in your report.

Here's where you let loose with that *unique sales proposition* we talked about earlier. That is…

> *"You know how others _____,*
> *well here's what I do that's different…"*

Without being arrogant, it's time to **talk about YOU**: your experiences, your knowledge, or your special way of doing things. You will also want to:
- Explain what you have to offer in your report that will help the reader to solve the problem they are facing.
- Tell a story to explain HOW you found out what you'll be sharing in your report.

YOUR HR GOLDMINE

- Empathize with the reader – let them know you've been where they were and tell them how things have changed since you made your discovery of what works.
- Point out what makes you different than the rest of those out there who might be offering similar products.
- Refer to tips, strategies, practices, etc. that you reveal in your report (without telling them exactly WHAT those items are, of course!)
- Mention specific results you've achieved by using the information included in your report.

You don't want to make claims, you want to PROVE them, which brings us to…

PART 6: YOUR PROOF

Anyone can make claims about what they've done and what they know, but how many can prove it? And, when they prove it, how much more effective is their claim?

People, in general, are naturally skeptical. Especially those who've been around the block a few times and have fallen for hype before. If you want to bridge the gap between their wallet and your order button, you've got to establish trust.

And the surest way to establish trust is to <u>prove</u> what you're saying is true.

The best way to validate your claims by providing **testimonials**. It's one thing when YOU say the information included in your report works…it's another thing entirely for someone else to proclaim the excellence of your report themselves. A testimonial from someone who's read, used and seen results from your report represents a voice of credibility speaking on your behalf. One or two testimonials should be sufficient for your report sales message.

To illustrate how persuasive this can be, here are two testimonials from my *Start Your Own Awesome HR Blog* report:

Amazingly detailed, HR pros will benefit from this information

"I can't wait to start my HR blog. I have considered blogging for sometime but have been overwhelmed with the thought of doing so. Blogging is not as complicated as it may seem and Alan proves this by doing a wonderful job guiding you through the process of creating a blog. Alan has amazed me with the amount of detail he has been able to provide in a downloadable report and the videos. Many HR Pros will benefit from this information."

Mark A. Griffin, founder InHisNameHR.com & former Vice-President Human Resources, VALCO Companies, Inc.

Guide on how to move from inspiration to action

"If you have ever had the slightest inspiration to begin blogging and getting your thoughts read by a large audience, Alan Collins' latest book, 'Start Your Own Awesome HR Blog' is a great "by-the-numbers" guide on how to move from inspiration into action. I've wanted to start my own HR blog and this book makes it easy for me."

Al Duff, Vice President – Human Resources, WMS Corporation

Testimonials can go a long way to tear down the wall of reluctance that rests between you and your potential customer. Also, notice how including the photos of the people whose comments you are using can further substantiate your claims and add legitimacy to your report.

When you've laid out your proof, it's time to get specific about what's included in your report, and that means it's time for...

PART 7: BENEFIT BULLET POINTS

A *bulleted list* of benefit points is one of the most effective ways to really drive home the *reason why* the reader would want to purchase your report.

It also allows you the opportunity to address **several different "angles"** of the information you include – one of which might be that special hot button with the reader that seals the deal.

You've seen them on just about every sales message.

As an example, here's a quick list of some of the bullet lists used in my HR blogging report...

- *How to <u>never run out of articles</u> and posts for your HR blog...this includes 40 ideas that you can borrow, steal or immediately reapply for your blog when you get stuck.*
- *The <u>#1 secret</u> for boosting your HR career using your blog...and seven ways to take advantage of this secret.*
- *How to <u>attract traffic and readers</u> to your blog. There are 500+ ways to generate traffic to your blog...but, your time is valuable...so, here are the 8 methods you should consider first.*
- *47 ways to <u>hook your readers</u> with every single post you put on your blog & keep them coming back to your blog for more.*

Three quick things I want to mention about these "points"...

Stress benefits, not features. The classic statement about benefits vs. features is this: "no one cares about your lawn mower, they only care about their lawn." Your report might very well have 10 ready-made training plans included... but what does that mean to the reader? It means they don't have to spend time developing the training plans themselves; it means they don't have to be in a rush; it means they can use their saved time doing something more enjoyable. A benefit is simply WHY the reader should care about your feature.

Stress particulars, not generalities. It's not "Helpful ways to...", it's "11 helpful ways to...". It's not "better time management," it's "cut the time you spend in unproductive meetings by 2 hours a day." The more specific you can be, the better. And, let me mention something that really adds credibility to your bullet points is to list a specific PAGE in which the information is found in your report. What I recommend is writing something like "(Page 7)" – after the bullet point so the reader can know exactly where to find what you've mentioned in that point. Very, very effective.

Stress majors, not minors. You should only use about 6 to 12 bullet points in your sales message -- so make them count. You want to stress the most desirable benefits to the reader ... the "major" helps included in your report. It's important that you fire your biggest guns. And try to focus on different aspects of the information you're sharing in the report. For example: one bullet point might focus on the *speed* in attaining results, while another bullet point might focus on the *ease* of attaining results, while another bullet point might focus on the *positive feedback from others* you'll get as a result of attaining the results, etc.

Now, after you've got 6-12 bullet points in place here, it's time for the next "part" of your sales message, which is...

PART 8: THE PULL

The pull is your *call to action.* You know the drill from every commercial advertisement you've seen on television...

"Operators are standing by ... place your order NOW!"

Don't delay. Quantities are limited. The next 10 callers get xyz. Yada, yada, yada. Blah, blah, blah.

While I'm certainly not a believer in using psychological mind games to prey on the emotions of readers to push them over the edge, it is important that you point them towards a decision. It is important that you instruct them to take advantage of your offer and place their order.

It's all about creating urgency. In other words, you don't want them to delay in making the decision to buy ... they might not ever be back again. *You've got their attention RIGHT NOW, so you want them to make their decision RIGHT NOW.*

Perhaps <u>the best way</u> to get them to do this is to impose some kind of deadline or limit which makes it necessary to order soon in order to take advantage of a special price, extra incentive or availability.

Special Price. By offering a discount to all who purchase within a specific period of time (or to a selected number of people who order -- i.e. The first 100), you can create a sense of urgency. This isn't going to be as useful to you as a writer of low-priced reports simply because, let's face it, the difference between the "regular" price of $15 and the "discount price" of $10 isn't substantial enough to be alluring.

Extra Incentive. You may want to consider offering an additional bonus (we'll talk more about this in an upcoming chapter) to those who order within a specified time or specific number. This CAN be an effective option for you to use. For example: If your report is about "setting up new orientation program" you might state, "The first 100 people who order will receive a free copy of an actual orientation program you can use as an example to guide you as you develop yours..."

Availability. Another option is to remove the report from circulation after a specified date or a specified number of units are sold. I don't like this one for obvious reasons: I'd like to sell as many copies as I can! However, one strategy that I do see merit in using is taking a report "off the market" for an unspecified period of time. In other words, you "retire" the report for several months and then bring it back later – or even add more information to it and convert it into a larger product. Or, another idea is to no longer make it available from your website and only offer it as a backend to a second report you create later, etc.

Now, a limit or deadline isn't as necessary for low-cost reports they are for full-scale, premium-priced products like books or audio programs ... so don't waste a lot of time on this.

I will give you two age-old, still-effective ways to "encourage" people to order that have "built-in" urgency:
1. The Rule of <u>Results</u>. Stated simply, "the longer you wait to get started, the longer it will be before you see results." The flipside is also true: "the quicker you get started, the quicker you'll see results."
2. The Rule of <u>Response</u>. The more people begin using this information, the less effective it can be. For example, if you're selling a report on recruiting chemical engineers, you could say: "As more and more people begin competing to hire highly talented chemical engineers, it's more difficult to get the top candidates to join your organization. A delay in taking action to order this report could diminish your effectiveness as others beat you to the punch."

By using these two "built-in" triggers to create urgency, you can reasonably point your site visitors to a buying decision without resorting to high-pressure sales tactics.

Speaking of pressure – the next "part" of your sales message certainly helps remove it...

PART 9: YOUR PROMISE.

In other words, your *"guarantee."* Risk reversal is the ultimate way to remove any remaining barriers between you and your potential customer. By risk reversal I mean making it clear that THEY have "nothing to risk." **If they are dissatisfied for any reason, you'll refund their money with no hassles.**

<u>Note</u>: It's important that you include any "terms" relevant to your guarantee. For example: how long does the customer have in order to obtain a refund should they choose to do so? In many cases, legally you must provide at least 30 days. And, depending on whom you choose to process your orders, there will be

requirements from those companies that you'll need to comply with. We'll talk more about that later.

The important thing is that you communicate to your site visitors that you are committed to their absolute satisfaction. Ultimately, they only pay for what they are pleased with having bought.

To illustrate, let me give you a quick look at great example of a guarantee...

100% Satisfaction -- 60 Day Money Back Guarantee:
Get your copy of "Start Your Own Awesome HR Blog" (and the bonuses) and try them all out. If you're not 100% satisfied, for any reason, I will refund your money anytime within 60 days of your purchase. No questions asked. No hassles. No drama. And we'll part friends!

And with that, let's move to...

PART 10: PROCESS

Finally, you're ready to take orders and start making money! (Congratulations, by the way! ☺)

You'll want to include three simple things here in this order process that are worth mentioning...

Last-Minute Instructions. Let them know how the order will be fulfilled (i.e. "Instant download"). Mention any bonuses they'll receive. If there are any special instructions (i.e. Register for free updates on the download page, etc.) then mention those as well.

Links. That is, your order link(s). I usually have the link read something like "Click Here to Order Now" or "Get Instant Access By Clicking Here" or some similar statement. Obviously, the actual link itself will need to lead to an order processor to accept payment on your behalf. This link will be provided by whatever processor you use to handle your orders ... which we'll talk about in our next chapter.

YOUR HR GOLDMINE

Legalities. Always, always, always include appropriate legal statements to protect yourself. More information on this topic is available at http://www.InternetLawProducts.com. Again, just make sure you have some kind of disclaimers and language in place on your website so that you're covered off legally.

So, here's an ideal example of what an "order process" portion of sales message looks like...

Click Here To Order

DOWNLOAD THIS CONFIDENTIAL
REPORT IMMEDIATELY!
(including all 3 Extra FREE BONUSES)

Simply click the order button above
make your payment & download
the Report & Videos!

You Pay Just $37.00

This special discount price is good
FOR A LIMITED TIME ONLY!
Start Your Own Awesome HR Blog and begin
the process of enhancing your own
Human Resources career...starting today!

YOU WILL RECEIVE INSTANT ACCESS
TO THIS REPORT AND ALL THE BONUSES
(Even if it's 2:00 AM on a Saturday)

*Every effort has been made to accurately represent this product and it's potential. Please remember that each individual's success depends on her background, dedication, desire and

> **motivation. As with any business endeavor, there is no guarantee that you will earn any money.**
>
> © Copyright by Alan Collins, SuccessInHR.com

And that brings us to the final "part" of your sales message…

PART 11: THE POSTSCRIPT

Immediately below your name at the bottom of your sales page should be a *postscript*. You know the drill, "P.S. Blah, Blah, and Blah".

Why include a P.S.?

Because people <u>WILL</u> read them. Sometimes they'll even jump to the bottom of the page and **read that first**. (They're usually looking for the price.) Regardless of the order in which they get there, *they will get there*. And they'll read your P.S.

So, since you'll have their attention at this point, it's important that you *make the most of it*.

Three powerful ways to finish strong in the sales process is to use your postscript to *"recap," "remind"* or *"reinforce"*…

RECAP the offer. That is, in ONE sentence, give a brief account of what the reader will be receiving when they place their order. (e.g. "P.S. This is a no-brainer: you'll get 3 years of talent management research boiled down to 22 pages of 'no-fluff' content in detailed, step-by-step format for only $19.")

REMIND them of a key benefit. Take a sentence to point out once again a desirable result the reader will experience by making the purchase (e.g. "P.S. Don't forget, in less than 24 hours you can actually be able to get up in front of your sales team and begin facilitating their off-site meeting with confidence…isn't that exciting!")

REINFORCE the call to action. Did you impose a deadline or limit? Did you mention an extra incentive? Did you pose a challenge? Use your "postscript" to reinforce some element of your call to action (i.e. "P.S. Unfortunately, when the remaining 17 copies are gone, this offer won't be repeated. Order now!")

(You will note on my website for *Start Your Own Awesome HR Blog,* I didn't include a P.S. as part of my sales message. My bad. It was a judgment call on my part. If I had to do it over again, I would include a P.S. However, since this report has been selling so well, I'm hesitant to mess with success!).

Alright, you've just been given a crash course in writing sales messages. If you include all 11 "parts" in your own sales message, you should have a terrific piece in place to convince visitors to your website to buy your report.

Speaking of your site, it's time to look at how to set it up so you can actually begin taking orders.

10

STEP SIX:
HOW TO P.U.T.U.P. A WEBSITE THAT WILL COLLECT & INSTANTLY DEPOSIT MONEY FROM YOUR CLIENTS…WITHOUT YOU NEEDING TO LIFT A FINGER

It's getting exciting now, isn't it?

You should have finished your report by this time. You've written your sales message. Now, it's time to put up a website that your customers can use to order your reports…and one that will automatically process payments for you and deposit them into your bank account.

So, that's what we're going to focus on.

Let me say this upfront: there are dozens of different options for setting up your website and using it to process your orders. I couldn't possibly give you a universal "step-by-step" look at every option available because the way things are done at each processor is different.

Therefore, in this chapter, I'm going to tell you WHAT you need to do, offer some suggestions on WHERE to do it, give you some ideas on HOW to do it. That should equip you to actually get it done regardless of the choices you make.

Sound fair? Good. Let's get started...

I use the acronym P.U.T.U.P. to explain the five steps for preparing and setting up your web site to sell and get paid your reports...

> P = <u>PICK</u> a domain name.
> U = <u>UTILIZE</u> web site hosting.
> T = <u>TIE DOWN</u> your order process.
> U = <u>UPLOAD</u> your files.
> P = <u>PREPARE</u> for your first order.

Let's take a closer look at each of these five steps...

STEP 1: <u>PICK</u> A DOMAIN NAME

The process of setting up your web site begins with selecting your own domain name. The price for registering a domain name is less than $10 per year at most registrars (I'll give you a recommendation in a moment), so it's not going to cost you much to get this done.

The key is to select the appropriate domain name. There are four characteristics of a good domain name for your report that I want to quickly mention...

Only choose a .com domain name. There are a gazillion different extensions available these days, but the primary one remains ".com". Unless there is a significant reason to do something else, I'd only recommend you choose a .com domain name.

Make your domain name easy to remember. Keep it as short as possible. Avoid dashes (Teambuilding-For-Managers.com). Avoid numeric substitutions (Teambuilding4Managers.com). Look for domain names that are short and easy to spell and you'll be in good shape

If possible, focus on keywords and use them in your domain name. For example: You'd have a better chance at getting ranked higher in google and other search engines for "Coaching" if your domain name is "CoachingSupervisors.com" than if it was "SupervisoryExcellence.com". While it's not necessary to become a search engine optimization wizard, it doesn't hurt to work things in your favor by simply including your keywords in your domain name.

Choose a "matching" domain name. That is, choose a domain name that is directly related to the title of your report. When I created my report, *"Create Your Own Awesome HR Blog,"* my keyword was "hr blog" so I chose the domain name "AwesomeHRBlog.com." Notice that it meets all of the above criteria.

Registering Your Domain Name

Now, there are many, many *"registrars"* online where you can pay to register a domain name for your exclusive use. Registrations are sold in yearly units.

The only one that I'd recommend is **GoDaddy.com.** At this time, they charge $10 a year to register a domain name. If you want to explore other registrars, you can do a google search for "domain name." However, GoDaddy has been great for me.

Once you've chosen your registrar, you'll then want to register your domain name there and get that settled. The registrar will then give you the option for *"nameservers."* When that happens, choose to have the domain *"parked"* with the registrar. You'll be able to change this after you select a web site hosting company which is what we'll cover next.

<u>Note</u>: Without going into too much tech talk, a "nameserver" simply points the domain name to the hosted web space so people can actually visit your site. That's a good thing. ☺

To illustrate this, type your domain name into the address bar of your favorite browser and click ENTER. What happens? You'll either arrive at a page that informs you the page you're looking for is not available; or you'll arrive at a page that informs you that the page you want is parked on behalf of your registrar. This is because, while you have a domain name, it isn't connected to any hosted web space at this point.

Let's move on to…

STEP 2: **UTILIZE** WEB SITE HOSTING

First, let's clarify: Think of your domain name as your "home address" on the internet….and web site hosting as your "land" on the internet. Every website online has both a domain name *home* and website host company that provides *land* for it to sit on.

You need both.

So, you want to look for a hosting company that offers the following list of features…

- Ample disk space.
- Ample bandwidth (data transfer).
- Ability to password protect directories.
- Acceptable "uptime".
- Great customer service.
- Web-based file manager.
- An easy-to-use control panel.
- Unlimited email accounts and aliases.
- Advanced features that you may use later: MySQL databases, CGI-bin, SPAM blockers, multiple domains, stats tracking, etc.

Now, there are literally hundreds, maybe even thousands, of hosting companies out there who will sell you web space to host your site for you. If you google the term "web site hosting," you'll find waaaaaay too many options to consider.

So, I recommend **HostGator.com.** This is the hosting company I use. These guys have THE best "offer" that I've seen for the price you pay. Every possible feature is available in their standard hosting package and their support team always responds QUICKLY to inquiries, even on weekends. If there's a better complete package available for their fee, I haven't found it yet. They get my highest recommendation. Please keep in mind that I do not get paid if you choose to use them. I simply recommend them on their own merits. I have found them to be a first rate choices for hosting. But, again, if you want to explore other alternatives just google: "web site hosting."

A word of warning: No matter what hosting company you decide to use, resist the temptation to use "free hosting" sites. The compromises you have to make with these kinds of web hosting sites just aren't worth it. Generally, they are slower, have poorer support and require you to place third party advertisements on your web site pages. Bottom line: you get what you pay for or what you don't pay for.

Now, after you order a hosting package with one of these companies, you'll be instructed on "nameservers." Generally, a nameserver will look something like this...

ns1.hostingoption.com
ns2.hostingoption.com

When you've been given this information from your hosting company, go back to your domain name registrar and login to your control panel provided to you. Change your default nameserver data to the information given to you by the hosting company. This will allow your website space to be *live* within 8-72 hours. When you type your domain name into your browser address bar, you will arrive at your space.

Congratulations! ☺

So, now that we've gotten this far, it's time to begin looking at your order-processing options.

STEP 3: <u>TIE DOWN</u> YOUR ORDER PROCESS

You need tie down and finalize a way to accept credit card and check payments online...without you needing to personally be involved in the transaction. This process needs to be instantaneous and efficient.

Again, as with most technology, there are many different options for your service provider. Vendors from all over the world are competing to get your business because they make money from you and the orders you process. They get a small percentage of every sale you make through their processing service.

This can make it difficult to select a third-party processor for beginners. Fortunately, I've been around the block more times than I care to remember, so I can certainly steer you in the right direction. Again, I don't make any money through these endorsements.

There are two recommendations that I offer for those wanting a "turnkey" third-party order processor…

Resource #1: Clickbank (www.Clickbank.com). I use Clickbank for just about all of my special report and e-book sites. They are probably the easiest third-party processor to get started with. There's a small one-time start-up fee ($49.95 at the time of this book). After that, they only charge you a small transaction fee ($1 + 7.5%) for every sale you make. That means if you're selling a $20 report you will earn about $17.50 profit! That's an 85% profit margin, which is awesome. You get paid for your orders twice per month on or about the 1st and 15th of each month. They automatically make deposits into your bank account. They even have a no-cost way for you to set up your own affiliate program so that thousands of other people in their data base can find out about your report and decide if they want to sign up as one of your "affiliates" and sell your reports for you for a cut of your profits (anywhere between 30%-70). Because of all these features, they are my top recommendation. They specialize in selling digital products like e-books, special reports, and downloadable PDF files so they're pros at this. Now, for security purposes, there are some steps you must complete to have your account activated and approved by them, but it's well worth it and it's all very straightforward and explained thoroughly on their site.

Resource #2: PayPal (www.Paypal.com). The reason I recommend them is because they have ZERO startup costs. If you are on a tight budget, they are a nice option because they don't require a setup fee to begin using their order processing service.

YOUR HR GOLDMINE

Their fee-per-transaction is among the lowest available, as well. Payment for the orders you generate is automatically deposited into your PayPal account. From there, you can choose to spend the money on a MasterCard debit card, get the money direct-deposited to your checking account or have a check mailed to you anytime you choose. You can sell digital products AND physical products with their service. There are some drawbacks with poor customer service and an itchy trigger finger when it comes to freezing accounts for violations of their Terms of Service, but still they are a very popular service that bears mentioning.

So, those are two quality options you have to choose from in selecting who you will use to process your orders.

Special Note: As mentioned on page 114, you can also get free payment processing services from **Amazon Kindle** if you use their publishing platform and decide to sell your report as a 20-40-page e-book. They operate the same way that Clickbank and Paypal do. However, starting out, I don't recommend them as a first choice because their 35-70% royalty is a whole lot less lucrative than the 95%+ royalty you'll get from Clickbank or Paypal.

Once you've selected an order processor…and have secured an account with them, login to the control panel they will provide you with and follow their detailed tutorials for setting up your report to sell. When you have done this, you'll be given an actual URL *"order link"* to place on your sales page.

From that point, there are a few minor things to do in finalizing your order process.

Create your SALES page. This is the primary page at your web site that will consist of your sales message that we spoke at length about in our last chapter. You will want to put a "Click Here" button on that site (or whatever you chose in writing your sales message page) to have that linked to the order URL provided to you by the third-party vendor you chose. Again, you can hire someone to setup the technical aspects of this for you should you choose not to do it yourself.

Create your FULFILLMENT page. The other accompanying web page you need to have created is your "fulfillment" page. This is the page at your site that your customers will be directed to after they have finished paying for your report. This page should include complete instructions on how to obtain the report they've ordered

Creating a download link is a relatively easy process. It requires marrying your domain name URL with the file name of your report. For example:

If TheCompensationSystem.com is your domain name. And your file name is "srnumbers.pdf", then your download link would be: TheCopySystem.com/srnumbers.pdf

The sales page and the fulfillment page are the minimum items you need in order to process an order at your site. Now that you have these two pages created, it's time for...

STEP 4: <u>UPLOAD</u> YOUR FILES

Uploading is the process by which you transfer files from your computer to your web site. Generally speaking, you have two options for uploading your files…

Option #1: Server. The best option to use is the file transfer function available through your hosting company. Every quality hosting service will offer this feature (especially Host Gator, which I recommended). You'll simply login to your hosting control panel and make the appropriate selection for uploading files directly to your site. Again, there should be ample instructions included in your control panel or hosting documentation to aid you in this very simple process.

With either of these options, make sure you "upload" the files to your MAIN directory at the site in order for the links to work properly as I've described. This is also known as your "root" folder or "public" folder or "WWW" folder.

The files that you'll want to upload are your...
- Sales page.
- Fulfillment page.
- Report.
- Applicable site graphics.

A word about graphics: If you – or the person creating your sales message page – used any graphics, pictures or images, then you'll need to make sure they are linked to and contained in your main directory and NOT in some "images" directory in order to properly view them. Or, you can create an "images" folder at your site, but this will take additional steps (albeit EASY steps).

Option #2: Software. There are several "FTP" software programs available that you can get which will be useful to your long-term business. The one that I use is "Filezilla" which is free at filezilla.com. It comes with complete instructions on using it and is a great tool to have. (*Note: There are many other transfer software programs available that you can find by searching google.*)

When you've "uploaded" files to your site, you're ready for...

STEP 5: PREPARE FOR YOUR FIRST ORDER

In this step, you *test* the entire process from start to finish in order to make certain everything is working properly.

Specifically, here is a quick checklist of things you'll want to do in order to verify the order process...
- Type your domain name into the address bar in your internet browser and click the ENTER button to visit the site.
- Upon arriving at your web site, verify that the page loads properly, with all images and text formatted in the desired layout.

YOUR HR GOLDMINE

- Click on your order link as if you were placing an order and verify that it transfers you to an order page with your third-party vendor.
- Verify that the information contained on the order page is correct, specifically the name of the product being ordered and the price for that product.
- Either place a real order or mock order to verify proper processing and delivery. If you choose, go ahead and complete the information needed to actually order the product. If you'd rather not, then type the fulfillment page URL For example:
  http://www.YourDomainNameHere.com/ty_dload.html.
- Verify that the fulfillment page loads properly with images and text formatted in the desired layout.
- Click on your download link and attempt to download the report file to your computer.
- Open the report file that you've just downloaded and make sure it is the correct version of your report and everything looks as planned.

If everything checks out properly, then congratulations, you're ready to take orders! If something does not work, make some corrections and try it again.

IMPORTANT REMINDER!

A SIMPLE SOLUTION IF YOU'VE NOT CREATED WEBPAGES BEFORE OR THIS SOUNDS ENTIRELY TOO COMPLEX…

Life's too short! As I first mentioned on page 116, using an expert will save you lots of headaches if you've not created web pages before. All this requires is simply outsourcing your webpage development to a web designer on elance.com. This is a $25-$30 job. You will want to give this web designer specific marching orders to create a finished page one page website that would contain:

YOUR HR GOLDMINE

> - *Your sales message*
> - *Any graphics you'll use on your site.*
> - *An order button* (linked to a url provided by Clickbank or PayPal so customers can order)
> - *An order fulfillment page* (where they will go to download your report after their payment has been received and processed)
> - *Your report* (in PDF form that they can download).
>
> That's all you need to have in place for an order-fulfilling website. If you need an example or model to follow, use AwesomeHRBlog.com.

After you've put up your site to sell the report as I've described here, all you need to now do is get visitors to your site to view what you have to offer.

So, with that in mind, now let's move to the next chapter.

11

STEP SEVEN: A BLUEPRINT FOR PROMOTING & BUILDING YOUR SECOND INCOME EMPIRE

It's now time to talk about the final step in the seven step process of profiting from your HR know-how.

While I've shared bits and pieces of this before – mostly to clients in private settings – this is the first time I've gone public with this information.

In this chapter, you're getting the *first look* at a very unique **6-phase blueprint** for creating a lucrative, potential six-figure income starting with just one, tiny well-written special report.

To that end, let's start with…

PHASE #1:
WRITE YOUR FIRST SHORT REPORT AND PROMOTE THE HECK OF IT!

Confucius said, *a journey of a thousand miles begins with a single step*. (Or something like that.)

And I say, *a journey to a lucrative second income based on your HR know-how begins with ONE single short report.*

YOUR HR GOLDMINE

So, phase one requires that you:

- Get that first report ready to sell.
- Write your sales message.
- P.U.T.U.P. your site.
- And then start promoting the crap out of it so you can see orders.

Here are four quick actions you can take to drive visitors (aka traffic) to your web site in order to begin generating orders.

Mention Your Report To Your Contacts. Begin with those with whom you already have a relationship. If you have an email list of contacts then the first order of business is to announce your report to it. Let them know that you've published a special report. In addition to this, set up a "signature" that appears at the end of all your outgoing emails. Example:

Susan G. Smith
9 Ways To Pass The HR Certification Exam in 21 Days or Less
www.PassTheHRCertificationExam.com

You might as well promote your report when you answer your emails! If you are involved in a "community" (i.e. SHRM, ASTD, OD Network, blogs, message boards, membership sites, mastermind groups, job transition groups, etc.) then use this signature at the end of your communications and postings to them also. Promote your short report to those in your immediate circle of contacts first. If you don't already have a contact list of some type, you need to begin building one.

Send Out Mailings Multiple Times To Your Existing Contacts and Clients. With your list of contacts, one of the biggest mistakes you can make is sending a mailing out ONCE, and then NEVER sending it out again. Continue to send out several additional broadcast mailings (each focusing on a different "angle" in its message) to your own lists. This never fails to produce more sales.

Write And Distribute An Ezine Article. Put together a few 300-400 word "ezine articles" (at ezinearticles.com). Allow others to use these articles to publish to their own lists and at their own websites, blogs, etc., to generate free publicity for your report. However, be use to include a "resource box" at the close of your article which announces your special report. This ezine article should be RELATED to the topic of your report. Send this ezine article to your existing contacts AND submit it for publication to other popular ezine article directories like GoArticles.com and others. I personally recommend that you use a service such as iSnare.com to handle these submissions for you as they can be quite time-consuming.

Leverage the Power of Social Media Sites To Promote Your Report. There are numerous ways to do this. Here are few of the most powerful:

(1) *Create a business Facebook page that your customers, prospects and fans can "like."* A separate Facebook page for your special reports enables you to create an opportunity for dialog with your customers and prospects. It also allows you to create related messages, post related videos from YouTube, and offer tips and ideas that will help your clients use the information in your report, build their careers and businesses, gain you a following…and help generate income. Most of your customers and prospects are probably already involved with Facebook, but likely only on a personal or social level. You can easily find them and ask them to like your page.

(2) *On Twitter, pull 15-20 key sentences from your report and turn them into tweets.* After each tweet, provide a link to the webpage containing your report. This will allow you have 15-20 different mini-messages you can

send out to your Twitter followers. You can rotate these messages and re-use them over and over.

(3) *Announce your new report to all the LinkedIn groups and forums that you belong to.* All of them have sections for announcing news items of interest to their members. Also join other LinkedIn groups and do similar postings. Repeat these postings a couple of times a month.

(4) *Begin interacting in LinkedIn groups on any discussion threads that are related to your report by posting insightful comments and pointing them to the website for your report...or by including your "signature" at the end of the post.* I'm sure there are numerous high-traffic LinkedIn discussion groups related to your topic where you can ask and answer questions related to your topic. For example: Suppose someone has asked a question in one of the HR groups such as, "It takes a lot of time to recruit job candidates using social media, how can I speed things up?" You would post a helpful reply and then insert a resource link for your report such as, "Click Here for 17 Ways To Quickly & Easily Use Social Media To Source Top Flight Job Candidates." Just like that, you're off and running. See how this works? Always deliver value by providing great insight in your answers and then steer the conversation to YOUR report. Make it applicable to the question or issue under discussion.

(5) *Create your very own LinkedIn group around the topic of your report.* With your own group, you have lots of freedom to ask questions, answer questions, create discussions, join discussions, ask for advice – and engage your group members around the topic of your report. In all of the interactions with your group members, you have an opportunity to promote the link to your report.

Create an affiliate program with Clickbank. By listing your report with Clickbank, you can easily create an affiliate program that allows others (called "affiliates") to sell your report in return for a commission – usually 30-50% of your price. This is like having your own army of sales people working to advertise your website and your report on a commission-only basis. It only takes a handful of good affiliates selling your report for it to begin generating some momentum and profits. You can also promote your Clickbank affiliate program to others in your target audience who are interested in generating an income from your report. To view an example of an affiliate program I've created, go to AwesomeHRBlog.com/affiliates.htm.

Dedicate Time To Learning One New Marketing Method Each Week. There are hundreds of ways to drive traffic to your report's web site. I would recommend that you spend a couple hours every week learning website promotion. Be careful not to get overwhelmed – and resist the temptation to go and buy every book or course out there that seems to be exactly what you're looking for. Set a budget for what you want to spend on your "education" and stick to it.

You can find helpful information on this topic by doing a google search for such phrases as...

"How to generate web site traffic"
"How to build an e-mail list"
"How to write an ezine article"
"How to promote on forums"
"How to use Adwords®"
"How to promote my site"

Or, by searching for free articles at some of the major ezine article directories like...

http://www.EzineArticles.com
http://www.Isnare.com
http://www.GoArticles.com

So, that's phase #1. Write and promote your first report. With that done, let's move on to...

YOUR HR GOLDMINE

PHASE #2:
CREATE 4-7 RELATED REPORTS AND CROSS-PROMOTE THE ENTIRE SERIES

Obviously, <u>ONE</u> short report isn't going to make you big money, unless it's very popular. So, let's take things up a level. In phase #2, you create 4-7 related reports and then cross-promote the series.

Let me give you a couple of "guidelines" first as recommendations before I talk about cross promotion.

Guideline #1: Make sure the additional reports you create are all "related" to each other. In order for this to really work well for you, each of your reports needs to be connected in some way so that when a customer buys one of them, they are automatically INTERESTED in the subject matter of all of them. The classic example here is "job hunting." Consider how someone in looking for their next job would have an interest in each of these related, but decidedly different, reports...
- A report on how to find your next job using LinkedIn.
- A report on the best ways of utilizing your personal network to generate job interviews.
- A report on how to turn job interviews into offers.
- A report on making yourself more attractive to headhunters.
- A report on how to negotiate the best salary possible.
- A report on how to succeed in the first 30 days in your new job.

Do you see how all of these are DIFFERENT, but they are also CONNECTED by their common bond? This dramatically raises the likelihood that your customer will make multiple purchases from this series ... perhaps even buying them all!

Guideline #2: Create at least one new short report per month, preferably two. How quickly you get to the more lucrative phases of this business is completely up to you.

YOUR HR GOLDMINE

My recommendation is that you create at least one additional short report per month. For this phase, you need a minimum of four reports, while the next phase will require that you have at least six short reports completed. At a rate of one-per-month, this would take you four months to complete this phase (#2) and six months to complete the next phase (#3). If you double your production to TWO short reports each month, you would reduce your time needed to complete these phases and really start to see significant progress.

However, one per month is fine. Two per month is optimal. Don't try for anything more or you'll be bombarding your contacts with TOO MUCH, not to mention you'd probably overtax and blow yourself up.

Now, as you create these additional reports, I want you to do everything I mentioned in phase #1 for each of them. In addition, add the following "cross promotion" steps as part of this phase...

Cross promote inside the reports themselves. In each of your reports include references to your other reports. You can do this in three strategic, yet subtle ways...
1. Include an "About the Author" page where you mention all of the reports you've written, along with links to your sales pages for each.
2. Mention the existing reports in the actual text if and when it is relevant. In other words, if you're talking about something that you've explained thoroughly in an earlier report, reference the report.
3. Create a "Recommended Resources" page to include at the end of your report which has a brief description and the web site links for all of your existing reports.

Every NEW report you create (at your ONE per month rate) should have these cross promotion points included – and updated to showcase ALL of your offers.

Cross promote on the "fulfillment" pages. Each of your reports has a "fulfillment" page as we've talked about earlier.

This is the web page where the customer downloads the report that they've ordered from you. This is a great spot for you to mention all of your other related reports by simply listing "Other Reports by <Your Name>." If you offer a discount for additional purchases, you should see an increase your orders.

Cross promote by using "upsell" pages. That is, you create an upsell page at your existing sales pages to offer additional reports.

Let's clarify: the normal sales process that we've covered already works like this: (a) Visitor clicks on your order link and arrives at your third-party processor and (b) Visitor places order and arrives at your "fulfillment" page.

By contrast, the "upsell" sales process works like this...
- Visitor clicks on your order link and arrives at an "intermediate" page.
- Visitor has two choices of order links.
    -Order only the original report.
    -Order a combination of two or more reports.
- Visitor makes their choice and places order.
- Visitor arrives at the APPROPRIATE "fulfillment" page.

In addition to the web pages that we've talked about in our earlier sections, you'll need to create an "intermediate order page" and an additional "fulfillment page" that has download links to the combination package being offered as the upsell.

You can find more information about this approach by going on google and doing some additional research. I just want to mention this as a great way to cross promote your series of reports.

Cross promote in your follow-up emails. You should always send emails to your customers "after the sale" thanking them for their order, etc. In these follow-up emails you can again make reference to your entire series of reports.

You can even provide the customers with your ezine articles sent out one per week that you've written to promote the reports. This will give you regular contact with your customers, provide them with additional free content and give you the continued opportunity to promote your series of reports.

I can't stress enough how profitable this type of cross promotion system can be. Not only are you SELLING each of these new reports, but they are automatically PROMOTING your existing reports which can create lots of additional orders.

So, once you've completed this phase – which should take from 2-6 months, depending upon how frequently you create new reports – it's time to move on to phase #3 which is when your sales and income can take a significant jump...

PHASE #3:
BUNDLE SEVERAL REPORTS INTO A HIGHER-PRICED PACKAGE.

At this point, you should be doing pretty well. However, one of the drawbacks up until this point is that YOU will primarily be doing all of the marketing yourself.

So, here's where things **change** in that regard.

If you have multiple reports, you should now be able to ATTRACT "affiliates" (see pages 149 and 156 for other references to affiliates and affiliate programs). These affiliates will be eager to help you promote your reports for a cut of the profits. So, instead of one person (you) doing all of the marketing, you can now enlist the talents of an entire virtual sales force to advertise your website.

However, you must make the profit split with them attractive. In other words, if you sell a report for $20 and pay 50% commission for sales referrals from affiliates and partners, that would only be about $10.00 per order. It would take a LOT of orders for the affiliate to earn any significant commissions from you.

And that's not enough. Affiliates are fickle. They go where the money is. If they can make $25, $50 or more per sale promoting something else, they'll certainly do that as opposed to promoting to earn a "cheap little $10 commission."

YOUR HR GOLDMINE

So I recommend that you...*take 6-7 of your short reports and bundle them into one package that sells for a higher price.*

If you've got 6 short reports that you've been selling for $20.00 each, that's $120.00 in value. Create a package that you offer for $77 or $97. That gives you something more lucrative for affiliates to promote and instantly gets you larger chunks of profit per transaction.

That means, instead of needing to sell 5,000 reports at $20.00 each to generate $100,000 per year, you only need to sell approximately 1,000 packages at $97.00 each to reach the same goal. That's significantly easier...especially when you factor in the efforts of an active group of affiliates.

Now, without trying to oversimplify things, there are a couple of steps you need to take in order to master this particular phase that I want to quickly mention...

You need to setup a separate website with a new sales message. This new website of yours will offer your $77-$97 package of reports. It will have its own domain name with its own sales message. In doing this, I strongly recommend that you don't simply say, *"Buy 6 of my reports for only a fraction of their total cost if sold separately"* That's a big, big mistake as far as the ability to convert visitors into paying customers.

What you want to do is create a totally new concept for the $77-$97 package of your reports. Think of your reports as part of an overall system of modules. Then write your sales message from the standpoint of no longer being ONE isolated report, but where all 4-7 reports now make up a complete "system."

Let me give you an example of this. When I was doing research for this book, there was a $197 course offered called: *The Information Products Creation System*. This course was nothing more than seven 30-40 page reports that covered the following topics:

- *How To Create An Information Product From Scratch*
- *How To Find The Best Topic For Your Information Products*

- *How To Hire Ghostwriters To Create Information Products*
- *How To Interview Others To Create Information Products*
- *How To Create Micro-Niche Information Products*
- *How Create Information Products Using Facebook and Twitter*
- *How To Create Information Products For Others For Fun & Profit*

What do all of these reports have in common? They are all DIFFERENT WAYS to create *"information products."*

Before, these were all sold as separate reports. Now they've been combined into one mega-package and offered at a premium price.

You can follow this exact same model. To do it, you need a separate website, with a separate sales message.

If you haven't started your affiliate program, you will definitely want to do it at this point. Your affiliates will love earning a 50% commission on your $77-$97 package and you should be able to attract tons of them.

One of the reasons that I recommend that you use Clickbank.com to process your orders is because they <u>automatically</u> set you up with an affiliate program for your account. They track orders. They award commissions based on the percentage you want. They pay your affiliates. It's all handled by them, not you.

With a bit of research on google and asking questions at one of the popular internet marketing forums (like for example the warriorforum.com, howtocorp.com/forum and ablake.com/forum you should be able to gather plenty of ideas for finding affiliates to promote your special package.

The important thing is that you bundle your existing RELATED reports into one package that you sell for a premium price and begin locating affiliate partners to advertise on your behalf.

Note: Also, be sure to provide your affiliates with each of those ezine articles you've written so they can publish them to their own lists and encode your resource box with their affiliate link. This gives them quality content they can use to endorse your package.

PHASE #4:
DEVELOP A BLOG AS A COMPREHENSIVE PROMOTIONAL VEHICLE TO SHOWCASE YOU AND YOUR REPORTS

By this time, you've turned your HR know-how into a big-time asset that you can showcase. It's now time to develop your presence online as a force to be reckoned with!

The best step you can take at this stage is to develop an on-line "*home*" that's all about you and what you offer. Your own blog can be "your face to the world" and the most effective entry way to everything you have to sell.

It's important that you create a blog for a couple of reasons:

People will begin to REFERENCE you as a TRUSTED AUTHORITY on your topic. As you become more and more prominent within your market, people will begin to talk about you – in a good way. They'll reference things you've said in your reports and your blog posts. They'll want to interview you. They'll point out things they've learned from you. They'll quote you. And you'll notice that they'll say things like, "Jill Smith *from* PerfectWorkplaceSolutions.com says…." There will come a day when you'll be "from" a specific web site. You'll be identified with that site and that will drive additional visitors to that site and to your reports.

People will begin to RESPECT you and you'll gain a FOLLOWING. People will want more and more of you. If they find something about your writing helpful and informative, they'll seek out other things you've written. By having a blog that showcases everything you offer, you'll give others the opportunity to purchase and assimilate as much of your materials as they choose. Good infopreneurs rarely find that customers only order ONE of their products...most order many.

So, having a blog is the next phase of expanding your second income empire. It doesn't need to be fancy. It just needs to include...

- A description of each of your reports as they are sold individually, along with a link to their respective web sites.
- A description of your "mega-package" offer with a link to its site.
- A listing of your free content available (i.e... The ezine articles you've been writing, etc.) with applicable links to their locations.
- A list to join (i.e. your newsletter) so that your target audience can receive regular emails from you.

If you need a model to follow for your blog, be check out mine at SuccessInHR.com. You notice how I use it to showcase my products on the right sidebar, along with other related products and a sign-up box so that they can receive regular e-mails from me. If you want more information on setting up your own blog, check out my 61-page special report: *"How To Create Your Own Awesome HR Blog."* (Sorry, I know it's a shameless plug, but I just couldn't resist!)

Now, before we move on to phase #5, let me share one more item that I want to mention separately because of the profound effect it can have on your business, now that you have your blog set up.

Here it is:

Create a "free newsletter" on your blog and use it promote EACH of your reports AND your mega-package.

Now that you've got several different products (i.e. individual reports and your mega-package) it's important that you effectively market them to prospective buyers.

One of the easiest ways to do this is to create a "free newsletter" that you offer on your blog. You can do with a series of email messages sent out at predetermined intervals through an autoresponder service like **aweber.com**.

Each of the issues of your newsletter would promote a different individual report or your entire mega-package.

A quick way to create a newsletter is to simply use the existing articles that you've already written. You can always create more later.

By adding this free newsletter your blog, you'll accomplish some very important things in growing your second income...

- You'll be able to build a list, which is an invaluable asset to your business as you start, sustain and strengthen relationships with subscribers.
- You'll be able to automatically promote everything you offer from one streamlined system.
- You'll be able to establish a brand, name recognition, and build a compelling "presence" online by regularly contacting your subscribers with each installment of the newsletter.
- You'll be able to add more messages to your newsletter long-term to promote your new reports as you release them.

There are many reasons why it's a good idea to have this newsletter. The bottom line is this: it will make you money.

'Nuff said.

Get your blog in the works at this phase, along with a newsletter that promotes everything you offer. When that's done, then it's time to continue advancing your business by moving on to...

PHASE #5:
"BULK UP" YOUR INDIVIDUAL REPORTS INTO FULL-BLOWN PREMIUM PRICED PRODUCTS

At this point in your business growth, it's time to begin further developing your individual reports. You can do this by converting each of your existing short reports, one at a time, into much larger products. This will allow you to sell them at a considerably higher price.

Now, there are a lot of different ways to do this, but the idea I like best is creating "kits" from your existing reports. The "kit" is my pet term for the technique of developing a report into a premium-priced product. Here are three ways to do it.

Kit #1 - Create 3-5 Simple, But Strategic Supplements. One of the things that separate reports from bulked up, full-size products is that the latter have related supplements. Whether these are *bonuses* or *accessories* or *modules*, the point is the same. You can turn your report into a bigger product by adding more "stuff." And, in doing this, you raise the perceived value which allows you to increase your price.

Now, let me be clear, I'm not talking about throwing in a bunch of worthless crap or rehashed stuff that you could pick up from anywhere. I'm talking about adding 3-5 supplements that enhance the VALUE of the information being shared in the report.

Some examples:

Checklists. One of the most popular supplements that you can create is the checklist. These are generally 1-3 pages in length and walk the reader through a chronological sequence of action steps to put into practice so they can master whatever was taught in the report. People love them because they can print them out and follow along, they can use them as a quick overview to follow the process and they can refer back to them over and over again. They are a must for any kind of short report.

Reference Lists. Another great supplement is a reference list. This would include swipe files, brainstormed ideas, a resource rolodex, contacts, categorized vendors, examples, case studies, style sheets, directories, journal entries, etc. A classic example is what was included with a report that focused on behavior-based interviewing. The report provided readers with 20 very specific interview questions, along with quick tips on how to sequence these questions in the interview, in order to better evaluate job candidates. Any kind of handy reference list that enhances or expands upon information shared in the report is a value-added supplement.

Forms. Does your short report require any kind of form? Would it be useful for the reader to have some kind of form in order to better benefit from your information? Great! Be sure to include one or more in your kit. Some ideas include: interview scripts, fill-in-the-blank templates, worksheets, form letters, lesson plans, letterheads, business card layouts, legal documents, evaluation forms, tracking sheets, journal pages, and so forth. Almost EVERY kind of report could be enhanced with some kind of form.

Tools. There are occasions when creating a small piece of software or some kind of web-based tool would be a great asset to include in your kit. Analyze your report and think about it from the reader's viewpoint. Would they benefit from having a piece of software? Consider these questions...

- Do readers need to collect data? (Ex. Contacts)
- Do readers need to track results? (Ex. Attendance, Accidents, Project milestones)
- Do readers need to automate a process? (Ex. Scheduling shift work)
- Do readers need to search for information? (Ex. Demographics)
- Do readers need to get organized? (Ex. Planner)

If you can answer "yes" to any of these, then I recommend you add a tool or have a small piece of customized software created to add to your kit as a supplement.

Of course, you don't have to create these software programs yourself. You can hire someone at Elance.com or RentACoder.com to do this for you. You can get very simple software programs developed for $200-$300, which is a no-brainer when it comes to adding value to your kit and ultimately increasing orders and profits. And, it will pay for itself in no time.

Coaching. This adds a tremendous amount of value as a supplement to your report. You could provide coaching in the form of:

- A critique of their approach to a problem that your cusomers e-mail to you.
- Individual personalized coaching from you (by phone, e-mail or in person).
- The ability to ask you questions anytime they want.
- An online forum where you (and others) can answer questions that are posed.

If you offer some kind of exclusive access where the customer can interact with you or others as it relates to helping them achieve the results they want from your report, you've got a winner!

So, that's the first of three "kits" you can create. In summary, it involves creating 3-5 simple, but strategic supplements to add to your report to make it bigger and better.

Kit #2 - Convert Portions Of Your Content Into Audio or Video. That is, record yourself reading the report and offer it as a downloadable audio file for your customers. Many people like to listen to information on their iPods, iPads, smart phones or on an audio player in their car while on the way to work, exercising or just relaxing.

They'd rather HEAR it than READ it.

And – let's face it – audio has a much higher perceived value than text. It always has and it always will. It just sounds more expensive.

So, I recommend that you convert your content into audio at a minimum and allow your customers to download it (along with the original report in PDF format) to their computers.

There are plenty of tutorials on how to create downloadable audio files available online ranging from free ones to low-cost products to premium-priced courses. You can search google or ask for a recommendation at warriorforum.com.

Now, there is also "video" to consider. If there are portions of your content that could be enhanced by a video demonstration, then that's another good idea for adding value to your "kit". Again, you can search or ask for information on how to make downloadable video files.

Most successful infopreneurs have been using downloadable audio and video files as a part of many of their courses for several years now and they are almost always a huge hit.

It's instant value added.

Okay, now there's one last "kit" that I want to talk about before moving on the next phase…

Kit #3 – Combine Your Short Report With Other Information. Obviously, if you want to increase your price, you're probably going to have to increase your information. That is, you'll need to <u>ADD MORE</u> content to your report to make it a larger work.

While there isn't any real "rule" to govern "how much more" content you need to add, I usually recommend at least 30 pages with an optimum being 50-75 pages.

Don't worry – it really isn't that difficult to take a 20 page report and bulk it up into 50 pages. Really, it isn't.

- You can add more content by expanding on each of the existing points you've made in your report as you explain them in greater detail.
- You can add more content by providing more examples, case studies and ideas for each of the existing points to better illustrate them.
- You can add more content by providing extra points in addition to the ones already shared in the report.
- You can add more content by introducing related topics and thoroughly explaining them as they fit with your existing content.
- You can add more content by offering "advanced" ideas for those wishing to "graduate" to a greater degree of knowledge or skill as it relates to your report topic.
- You can add more content by using "padders" such as quotes, charts, screenshots, stories, statistics, research, etc.

YOUR HR GOLDMINE

- You can add more content by using existing content from other people such as articles, excerpts, interviews, etc. – with their permission, of course.
- You can add more content by asking for questions related to your short report that you answer in great detail as additional information.
- You can add more content by introducing potential problems and offering suggestions on how to prevent and / or overcome these obstacles.

I've just given you 9 quick suggestions on what you can do in order to add more content to your report. I'm going to give you a 10th one in just a moment after I explain something here.

I want you to think about some of your additional content in terms of a *"part 2"* of your existing report. Now, the easiest way to offer a part 2 of any product is to use the *"basic to advanced"* model.

I actually have on my bookshelf a book entitled, *1001 Jokes For All Occasions,* and right next to it is a book by the same author that I bought when it was recently released entitled, *1001 More Jokes For All Occasions.* You should always have "part 2" information to include as you grow your existing report into a full-size premium product.

Now, you may not have noticed it, but I've just illustrated the 10th way you can add content to your report and that is to *recycle portions of your existing content.*

While you don't want to overdo this, there's nothing wrong with taking excerpts of your existing materials (other short reports, interviews, articles, newsletter issues, forum posts, blog posts, etc.) to quickly add as more content to your report.

Simply repeat this process of converting your short reports into full-length products for EACH of your existing reports. My recommendation would be to work on ONE conversion each month. That's going translate into a huge boost in your income.

But, it gets even better as we move into the final phase...

PHASE #6:
USE YOUR EXISTING REPORTS AS THE BASIS FOR TOP TIER, HIGH-TICKET INFORMATION PRODUCTS

When you arrive at this final phase, you'll already have a thriving second income empire, so congratulations on that.

But, that's **not the pinnacle!**

The pinnacle is located at the top of *Mount High-Ticket Product.* Those that climb to the top of this mountain are in a select few. They are in a group by themselves and they usually make an awful lot of money.

Ready to begin that climb?

Good, because the way you do it is quite clear: *use your existing reports as the basis for creating "top tier" information products.* The big three of the top tier are:
1. Physical Products
2. Live Events
3. Subscription sites

Let's discuss each of these one by one.

Top Tier Product #1: Physical Products. You've undoubtedly seen them before: products consisting of 3-ring notebooks, spiral binders, CDs, DVDs and so forth. These are "physical" products and they command a premium price.

The point is this...

There are much higher profit margins in delivering your content in formats other than reports or even books.

What has a higher perceived value: a book or a package of notebooks and CDs? Obviously, the latter.

This is the approach for creating premium, high-ticket products. You want to increase the perceived value of your product which allows you to increase the price you charge for it.

Now, there are a lot of different options for delivering this type of content other than a special report. Things like...

- Videos
- Workbooks
- Assessments
- Printed manuals
- 3-ring binders
- Complete toolkits
- And so forth.

Obviously, covering each of these in-depth is beyond the scope of this book. At this point, I just want you to realize that you have options other than reports for delivering your content that are potentially much more profitable.

The Easy Way to Double The Price Of Your Product

If you don't want to do a lot of extra work in creating a different format for your product, then you can at least record yourself reading the entire product and then burning it to a CD that you ship to your customers.

This is a simple way to double the price of your product that costs only 30-40 cents if you create a CD and stick it in a jewel case, which can easily be self-funded with a shipping and handling charge.

Many people PREFER to "listen" instead of reading (as I mentioned earlier), especially those who are on the road a lot.

Audio books are some of the most popular items of our time, and since they are so easy to create ... why not offer one for your product?

Who wouldn't want to double their profit when it's this easy?

Print out your product and convert it into a spiral bound manual and you've got even greater value added to the package.

See how easy this is?

Here's another alternative: You could also create a 2nd CD with a PDF transcript of your audio on it – which is basically the original product before you recorded it. It could include some other related reports, articles, bookmarks and resources to add even more perceived value.

YOUR HR GOLDMINE

Suddenly you've got a 2 CD set that's more of a toolkit than it is an audio book and again your premium pricing increases with the perceived value.

It's all about delivering the same content that you're going to distribute anyway – in a new, premium package that commands a higher price tag.

I mean, why would you want to charge $20 for the same content that you could sell for $49 or even more?

What you need to know is this: Nothing about your effort in producing sales is going to change regardless of how much you charge for your product.

The effort that you take to generate traffic is the same.

The effort that you take to secure customers is the same.

The effort that you take to make the sale is the same.

Why not make more money doing what you're going to do anyway?

And, really, there are a couple of additional benefits that are worth mentioning here.

Benefit #1: With a higher profit margin you can raise your visitor value which means you can actually pay more to generate leads, giving you yet another advantage over those who are competing against you.

Benefit #2: And, as we've talked about earlier, by offering a product that sells for a higher price, you are more likely to attract affiliates to promote your offer for you. If your competition is selling a product for $20 that pays out 50% and you're selling an equally as good product that converts well for $49 that pays out 50%, which one do you think affiliates are going to devote their time and effort to promoting? They are obviously out to make the most money they can make, so you again gain the advantage.

One more thing I want to mention before we move on. If you have a physical product like a CD or a workbook, you can actually charge a shipping and handling fee that covers the cost of duplication, so there isn't any more expense than there would be if it was a digital product.

It's just a no-brainer in my book. It just makes sense and it just makes more money.

YOUR HR GOLDMINE

Top Tier Product #2: Live Events. These would consist of e-coaching, seminars, or e-classes. Again, we're talking about packaging your content in higher-quality formats.

Look at the differences here just to illustrate why this is such a big money generator...

You can offer a 4-chapter product that might sell for $47.00 with some bonuses and other "supplements" that we talked about earlier.

You can tweak that content just a bit to make it interactive. Then you can offer it as a 4-week e-coaching program (one chapter per week) where the customer turns in assignments that you grade. By personally interacting with them in this way, you sell basically the same content for 5-10 times the price.

The same thing goes for a one or two day workshop. Or, a teleseminar. Or a webinar.

I'll reiterate something that I mentioned earlier, that is also applicable here...

People pay a premium price for <u>interaction</u> and personalized <u>attention</u>.

Mark that down. Circle it. Underline it. Make sure it sinks in. It's that important.

The third type of "top-tier" that I really consider to be a mandatory part of every information business by phase #6 is...

Top Tier Product #3: Subscription Sites. These are continuity or subscription programs where members pay you a recurring fee (either monthly, quarterly or yearly). These types of programs provide incredible streams of extra income.

I know of an HR guy (who asked me not to use his name) who is an infopreneur in the executive coaching niche. He is a full-time senior HR executive in a Fortune 500 company and creates training products on the side that help consultants and executive coaches of all skill levels improve their game. He offers reports, DVD's and a monthly continuity membership. His

YOUR HR GOLDMINE

membership site has 500+ paying subscribers month in and month out. Each member pays $17 per month for the content.

Now let's do the math on this: 500 subscribers at $17 a month equals a guaranteed $10,500 a month income. The brilliant part of this strategy is that the monthly content only has to be created once, and can be used for years to come. At the time of this writing, his coaching business had 21 months of content in the queue for subscribers. At $10,500 a month- that's a whopping $126,000 in annual revenue just from the continuity portion of his site!

So, that's why it's so critical that you consider putting together a subscription site where you create residual income for yourself.

The simplest way to do this is to setup a subscription site where you offer ONE new "short report" per month related to your topic of expertise.

Just record it as an audio and offer it as an "audio newsletter" if you want.

The important thing is this: Over a period of time you'll add a huge chunk of profit to your bottom line as more and more members join and remain active for months and even years to come.

Now that you know how to promote and grow your second income empire starting with just one, single report, I'll now summarize everything for you and pull it together in one plan.

12

THE STEP-BY-STEP PLAN FOR GETTING EVERYTHING LAUNCHED IN JUST 7 DAYS!

At this point, you probably feel like you've just taken a drink from a fire hose.

I understand fully. We've covered a lot of information. So, in this chapter I'm going to pull all this together for you in a **simple, step-by step 7-Day Plan.** By completing this plan, which is in the form of a checklist, you'll be able to start from scratch (with absolutely nothing – not even an idea!) and actually be ready to take orders in exactly seven days.

Each day's assignments will take approximately 2-4 hours depending upon your speed in completing them. You may work strictly by the schedule (i.e. complete the day one assignment on day one), get ahead of the schedule (i.e. complete the day one assignment and day two assignment on day one) or even lag behind the schedule (i.e. complete the day one assignment over the course of days one and two). Bottom line: This is YOUR guide – for you to use to work at whatever pace that works best for you!

Each of the daily assignments is arranged in a user friendly, strategic format…

- Assignments appear in chronological order based on what you need to do first, second, third, etc.
- Assignments comprehensively cover the entire process of creating a short report from start to finish.
- Assignments will reference specific chapters in this book that provide detailed instructions on how to complete that assignment.

The chapter you're in right now is one that you'll want to make copies of so that you can "check off" the assignments as you complete them. So take just a minute to do that now.

After you have a hard copy printed, let's begin.

DAY 1:
MAKE YOUR FOUNDATIONAL DECISIONS

Today's assignments will focus on setting up your foundation upon which you will develop your first report.

STEP 1: Decide upon a "target audience" that you will focus on serving. (See Chapter 4)

- ☐ Is it a target audience accustomed to spending money?
- ☐ Is it a target audience that can be presented with a variety of offers?
- ☐ Is it a target audience you are personally attracted to?

<u>Note:</u> *Refer to the list of 90+ audiences and markets in Chapter 4 to guide your decision making. Feel free to steal directly from this list if you are creating a report for the first time.*

STEP 2: Determine the topic of your report. (See Chapter 5)

- ☐ Look for a topic with *"demand"* –
  - Check out Clickbank's Marketplace.
  - Scan the best-sellers list at Amazon.com related to your topic.

- Do a google search of your topic to see what your "competition" has created in the form of books, e-books, special reports, white papers, etc.
- Look in the online message boards and discussion forums related to your topic for "hot issues" that might lend themselves to special report ideas.
- Look in popular article directories like ezinearticles.com for articles on your topic.
- Find offline magazines related to your topic.

☐ Look for a topic with *distinctiveness* –
- Segmented (i.e. A very narrow "niche" topic)
- Supplemented (i.e. A list of many different related ideas)

<u>Note</u>: *Don't forget to refer to the 157 HR Topic Ideas in Chapter 5 for additional thoughts on "what" to write about AND also Chapter 8 for ideas on "positioning" your report.*

STEP 3: Choose a title for your short report. (See Chapter 6)

☐ Does the title *Accurately Represent*?
☐ Does the title *Build Interest*?
☐ Does the title *Communicate Benefits*?

<u>Note</u>: *At this point, I recommend that you register the domain name and secure hosting (the next two steps) for your report on day one so you can "lock it up" and have it ready for you to go "live" with your order-taking when you are ready. However, if you're still undecided on a domain name or a host company, you can delay both of these decisions until Day 7 in this plan (when it WILL be time to put up your website)...but this will pack a lot of activities into this final day, which might necessitate going to an 8th day of the 7 day plan. Obviously this is*

not a big deal in the overall scheme of things, but just wanted to give you a heads up.

STEP 4: Register the domain name for your report. (See Chapter 10)

- ☐ Only choose a .com domain name.
- ☐ Make your domain name easy to remember.
- ☐ If possible, focus on keywords.
- ☐ Choose a "matching" domain name.

Note: Recommend using GoDaddy.com for registering your domain name.

STEP 5: Secure web hosting for your report. (See Chapter 10)

- ☐ Verify that the web hosting company has the features you'll need.
  - Ample disk space
  - Ample bandwidth (data transfer)
  - Ability to password protect directories
  - Acceptable "uptime"
  - Great customer service
  - Web-based file manager
  - An easy-to-use control panel
  - Unlimited email accounts and aliases
  - Advanced features that you may use later: MySQL databases, CGIbin, SPAM blockers, multiple domains, stats tracking, etc.

Note: My #1 hosting recommendation is HostGator.com

- ☐ Update your "nameservers" after securing your web hosting. (See Chapter 10)

YOUR HR GOLDMINE

DAY 2:
OUTLINE AND DIVIDE YOUR CONTENT INTO THREE WRITING ASSIGNMENTS

Today's assignment will focus on preparing your detailed outline for writing your report over the next three days.

> Note: Beginning with today's assignments you will be using the P.A.G.E.S. system as outlined in Chapter 6.

STEP 1: Brainstorm ideas for possible inclusion. (See Chapter 6)

- ☐ Write down everything you can think of related to your topic.
  - Ideas
  - Notes
  - Lists
  - Questions
  - Reminders
  - Personal reflections
  - Thoughts
  - Things-To-Do
  - Checklists
  - Details
  - Steps
  - Facts
  - Reasons
  - Comparisons
  - Contrasts
- ☐ Use the "alphabetizing" exercise in Chapter 6.

STEP 2: Arrange your ideas into a workable outline (see Chapter 6)

- ☐ Sequentially. (i.e. arranged in chronological order.)

YOUR HR GOLDMINE

- ☐ Systematically. (i.e. grouped together by logical relationships.)

STEP 3: Decide upon a "goal" number of pages to write. (See Chapter 6)

> Example: Let's suppose you want to create a 20 page report. Let's further suppose that you have 40 "ideas" that you've brainstormed to share in the report, arranged in 5 different sections. Doing the math, you will need 1/2 page of content per idea in order to meet the page requirement. So, begin writing the first point and when you've reached 1/2 page, you can quit anytime you finalize that idea.

STEP 4: Divide your writing into 3 daily assignments.

- ☐ **PAGES** - If you have 20 pages that you want to write, then each daily writing assignment would need to include completing at least 7 pages of content.
- ☐ **POINTS** - If you have 24 points that you want to write, then each daily writing assignment would need to include completing at least 8 points.
- ☐ **PARTS** - If you have 3 parts that you want to write, then each daily writing assignment would need to include completing at least 1 part.

DAY 3:
COMPLETE WRITING ASSIGNMENT NUMBER ONE

Today's assignment will focus on completing the first 1/3 of the content for your report.

STEP 1: Complete the writing portion scheduled for today.

- ☐ Write 2-4 paragraphs for each of the "points" in your outline.
- ☐ Be sure to thoroughly explain your ideas.
- ☐ Work in as many tips as possible.
- ☐ Include examples and case studies to illustrate your points when applicable.
- ☐ Inject your personality into the writing.
- ☐ Insert additional ideas and sub-ideas as they come to you. (They will!)

STEP 2: Use "content templates" #1 and #2. (See Chapter 6)

- ☐ If I could sum up <blank> in <blank> steps, here is what they would be <blank>.
- ☐ One of the things that the majority of folks find most challenging about <blank> is <blank>.

STEP 3: Extract "bullet points" for your salesletter. (See Chapter 6)

- ☐ Choose 10-12 of them as you make your way through writing the content.
- ☐ Compile them into a separate document for easy access later.

<u>Note</u>: *The assignments for days 3, 4 and 5 will be virtually identical.*

DAY 4:
COMPLETE WRITING ASSIGNMENT NUMBER TWO

Today's assignment will focus on completing the second 1/3 of the content for your report.

STEP 1: Complete the writing portion scheduled for today.

- ☐ Write 2-4 paragraphs for each of the "points" in your outline.
- ☐ Be sure to thoroughly explain your ideas.
- ☐ Work in as many tips as possible.
- ☐ Include examples and case studies to illustrate your points when applicable.
- ☐ Inject your personality into the writing.
- ☐ Insert additional ideas and sub-ideas as they come to you. (They will!)

STEP 2: Use "content templates" #3 and #4. (See Chapter 6)

- ☐ A little known secret about <blank> is <blank>.
- ☐ Perhaps one of the biggest reasons people fail in <blank> is <blank>.

STEP 3: Extract "bullet points" for your salesletter. (See Chapter 6)

- ☐ Choose 10-12 of them as you make your way through writing the content.
- ☐ Compile them into a separate document for easy access later.

DAY 5:
COMPLETE WRITING ASSIGNMENT NUMBER THREE

Today's assignment will focus on completing the final 1/3 of the content for your report.

STEP 1: Complete the writing portion scheduled for today.

- ☐ Write 2-4 paragraphs for each of the "points" in your outline.
- ☐ Be sure to thoroughly explain your ideas.

- ☐ Work in as many tips as possible.
- ☐ Include examples and case studies to illustrate your points when applicable.
- ☐ Inject your personality into the writing.
- ☐ Insert additional ideas and sub-ideas as they come to you. (They will!)

STEP 2: Use "content template" #5. (See Chapter 6)

- ☐ The one thing I always get asked about <blank> is <blank>.

STEP 3: Extract "bullet points" for your salesletter. (See Chapter 6)

- ☐ Choose 10-12 of them as you make your way through writing the content.
- ☐ Compile them into a separate document for easy access later.

DAY 6:
PUT ON THE FINISHING TOUCHES

Today's assignment will focus on preparing, packaging and pricing your report document for distribution.

STEP 1: Prepare your report document. (See Chapter 6)

- ☐ <u>PAD</u>: Insert additional content where needed to strengthen.
- ☐ <u>POLISH</u>: Use various fonts, font styles, indentions, separators, etc.
- ☐ <u>PROOFREAD</u>: Identify and correct grammatical and typographical errors.

STEP 2: Package your report document. (See Chapter 8)

YOUR HR GOLDMINE

- ☐ Contents –
    - Title page.
    - Legal page.
    - Author page.
    - Special offer page. (Discount | Deal | Deadline)
    - Table of contents.
    - Report.
    - Backend page.

- ☐ Cosmetics –
    - Header and footer.
    - Margins.
    - Fonts.
    - Headlines.
    - Indentions and boxes.
    - Styles.
    - Colors | Highlights.
    - Graphics | Screenshots | Photographs

<u>Note</u>: Compile your report and convert it into a PDF format. See Chapter 8 for details.

STEP 3: Price your report. (See Chapter 8)

- ☐ Rule #1 - *"Your content is the most important factor in determining price."*
- ☐ Rule #2 - *"Your competition's inadequacies help place a premium on your content."*
- ☐ Rule #3 - *"Your customer's expectations, buying habits and desires make the final decision."*

<u>Note</u>: The table on the next page illustrates a "general" rule of thumb for pricing without taking into the consideration the above listed rules.

Length of Report	Your Price
20-25 pages	$10 - $20
25-30 pages	$20 - $30
30-40 pages*	$25 - $40

*Anything more than 40 pages is no longer a short report, it's a manual or a short book.

DAY 7:
CREATE YOUR SALES MESSAGE AND PUT UP YOUR WEB SITE

Today's assignment will focus on setting up your order processing system to begin selling your report.

STEP 1: Write the sales message for your report. (See Chapter 9)

- ☐ Decide how your one-page website (that will contain your sales message) will be created.
- ☐ Write your sales message for your website to include the following 11 components –
  - Pre-Headline
  - Primary Headline
  - Post Headline
  - Problem
  - Product
  - Proof
  - Points
  - Pull
  - Promise
  - Process
  - Postscript

YOUR HR GOLDMINE

Note: Upon completing your sales message, have someone else proofread it for grammatical and typographical errors.

STEP 2: Create your order fulfillment pages. (Chapter 10)

- ☐ Create your one page website. (This contains your sales message with full graphics, formatting, etc.)
- ☐ Create your order fulfillment page. (This is your "download" page where customers access your report.)

Note: Included in the information on page 68 is a quick overview of how to establish download links to deliver your report to your customers upon purchase.

STEP 3: Upload your files to your web space. (See Chapter 10)

- ☐ Choose a method of transferring files.
    - Option #1: Software.
    - Option #2: Server.
- ☐ Transfer the following files –
    - Sales page.
    - Fulfillment page.
    - Report document.
    - Applicable site graphics.

STEP 4: Establish your order-processing. (See Chapter 10)

- ☐ <u>CHOOSE</u> a vendor to process your orders.
    - Recommended Resource #1: Clickbank.com
    - Recommended Resource #2: Paypal.com
- ☐ <u>COMPLETE</u> an account application with the chosen vendor. (i.e. You'll visit their site and complete the enrollment process to receive your account.)
- ☐ <u>CREATE</u> an order link. (i.e. Login to your provided control panel and create an order link according to provided instructions.)

Note: *The reason that I waited until the final day to establish your order process is because many companies (Including my top recommendation, Clickbank.com) require you to have your entire sales process in place prior to them approving your account.*

STEP 5: Test the process for potential problems. (See Chapter 10)

- ☐ Type your domain name into your browser.
- ☐ Verify that the page loads properly.
- ☐ Click on your order link and verify transfer.
- ☐ Verify information on the order form is accurate.
- ☐ Place a real or mock order to verify proper processing and delivery.
- ☐ Test the download link to verify proper path.
- ☐ Open the downloaded report to test correctness.

Final Thoughts

Congratulations! You're now ready to begin taking orders for your report. Please refer to Chapter 11 to begin marketing your new product.

Don't forget to continue building your report business using the "six phases" also described in Chapter 11.

13

HOW TO GET THIS DONE WHILE KEEPING YOUR DAY JOB IN HUMAN RESOURCES

You now know what being an HR infopreneur involves. You also know that the fastest and easiest way to become one is by packaging, promoting and profiting from your HR expertise utilizing short written reports (or *ebooks* or *white papers* if you prefer using one of those terms instead). We've also covered how to grow these short, packaged information products that you've created into a mega second income.

Let's now discuss how to accomplish all this while keeping your main gig. I'll start by giving you my basic premise…

If you are dependent upon the primary income from your full-time HR job, I'm a strong proponent of NOT doing anything to jeopardize it. This job pays your bills and is your security net right now.

Yes, I know that's common sense, but it needs to be said. To ensure that this happens, there are some rules you must follow to ensure that you don't put this primary source of income (or your sanity) in jeopardy while you work on tapping into your HR goldmine on the side. Here are those rules:

1. Know exactly where your current employer stands – don't assume anything.
2. Once you know where your company stands, decide how to deal with them and your boss.
3. Don't use (or steal) anything that belongs to your employer in your infopreneuring endeavors.
4. Do not write about anything that compromises or disparages your employer.
5. If your boss or employer absolutely will not support your infopreneuring endeavors, then go to plan B.
6. Be ready to sacrifice a lot of your personal time.

Let's discuss each of these in detail.

RULE #1:
KNOW EXACTLY WHERE YOUR CURRENT EMPLOYER STANDS - DON'T ASSUME ANYTHING

Think about two employers: A and B.

Employer A...is a big, traditional "old school" organization that doesn't share your enthusiasm for infopreneuring. In fact they believe they own you and your HR expertise, as long as you work there. They want your 100% loyalty...on and off the job, 168 hours per week...even though they're unprepared to provide you that kind of loyalty in return. By paying you an annual salary and other benefits, they feel are entitled to "first dibs" on your time and your ideas. They don't consider it slavery, because you are free to pack up and leave at any time, with no further obligation to them.

While you work there, they don't want you branding yourself in any way that could shed a negative light on them. So, they have written policies prohibiting moonlighting and running side businesses, without company permission. They perhaps even had you sign an employment agreement with a non-compete provision and which gives them (not you) the rights to any company-related intellectual property. This would include things like your special reports or other information products you created during company time or on their watch.

Unfortunately, that's not all they do. With more employees using social media, they are hyper-sensitive about protecting their brands and trade secrets. So they'll do (or pay for someone else to do) random, periodic social media background checks on you and other employees to ensure that you aren't positioning yourselves on Google, Twitter, LinkedIn, or Facebook as perverts, political extremists, or weirdoes. Just like you can catch a cold, organizations don't want to fall victim to the contagion that is stupidity on the internet.

That's employer A, obviously a worse case situation.

By contrast, let's look at the other end of the spectrum...

Employer B...is the enlightened, "new skool" organization. In these types of companies, performance rules. In their view, as long as you kick butt on your job, what you do on your own time doesn't matter to them...as long as you don't disparage the organization or compromise their main line of business. In these companies, you have people highly engaged away from work. Some teach in the evenings. Some run small unrelated businesses on the side. Some participate in non-profit organizations. Some coach and do non-competitive consulting.

Now, here's the question for you: Do you work for Employer A or B...or in a company that's a little bit of both?

You must know the answer to this question.

If you're not sure, check your employee handbook, your legal department or the corporate policy on moonlighting and running side businesses. Also, examine any employment documents you may signed when you began working in case you have agreed not to work with anything that conflicts or competes with your employer. If you're NOT certain, then ASK!

You will want to find out specifically:
- Does your company have guidelines?
- Is earning an income or running a side business acceptable?

- Are there topics that are off-limits?
- What are the consequences?

You want to go into infopreneuring with your eyes completely wide open and armed with all the facts.

RULE #2:
ONCE YOU KNOW WHERE YOUR EMPLOYER STANDS, DECIDE HOW TO DEAL WITH THEM AND YOUR BOSS.

You deal with your company primarily through your boss. And there are only two ways to handle your boss. You either tell your boss or you don't. Only you can assess your situation, but in most cases I recommend that you be…

Totally Upfront With Your Company And Your Boss!

Sure, you could hide what you're doing by using a pen name or a secret identity. That is, operate like Clark Kent during the day but then turn into Superman during the evening (or vice-versa). After all, some of the best authors in history have ghostwritten their best stuff under pen names. Mark Twain and Stephen King are two names that readily come to mind.

But the big problem with concealing your identity is that if you get found out, it gives the impression that you're trying to hide something. Or that you're subtly looking for work elsewhere. That's not exactly the kind of move that will enhance your HR career or your job security at your day job.

Also, if you can't use your own name as an infopreneur, what's the point? It doesn't help you build your personal credibility online as authentic brand and will limit your ability to build the kind of personal rapport that will increase the demand for your HR know-how.

So, because of these reasons, I believe it's best to be completely upfront and tell your boss what you're doing.

YOUR HR GOLDMINE

There are lots of ways of communicating this. Here's one example of a few talking points you might integrate (at the right time) in a lunch meeting with your boss:

> *"Hey, boss. I thought I'd share something with you that I'm excited about. I have a hobby. It's not golfing. It's not gardening. It's not buying and selling antiques. It's not stock trading. It's writing and sharing my HR wisdom in a way that informs, inspires and motivates others...and that does not jeopardize my job. I do it a few hours a week in my spare time."*

> *"I don't write about anything that relates to or disparages the company. I just wanted you to be aware of what I'm doing just in case you or the ABC Company has any concerns about it."*

There! You've laid your cards on the table. It's up to the boss to make the next move. Your boss may want to know more. She may want to see examples of what you're doing. To CYA, she may need to check in with Legal or the higher ups. Resist the urge to say "it's none of your business." Be upfront and provide any information required.

Now, I will tell you from personal experience that it is not comfortable having that kind of conversation with your boss. And, obviously the worst case scenario is that the boss and the company are not supportive of what you're doing...and if that's the case, don't despair, I'll cover what you do in that case (your Plan B) in Rule #5 coming up shortly.

RULE #3:
DON'T USE (OR STEAL) ANYTHING THAT BELONGS TO YOUR EMPLOYER IN YOUR INFORPRENEURING ENDEAVORS.

Yes, I know this is obvious. But it bears repeating. Don't use your company's computers, its network or do anything on com-

YOUR HR GOLDMINE

pany time. Resist the urge to stock your home office with supplies from your day job to use in your infopreneuring activities. Those are big no-no's.

In most companies, this kind of misuse of company property is considered theft and you can expect to be reprimanded or let go. Sure, you can rationalize this theft by saying "hey, the company can afford it." But since misappropriation of company property and office supply theft accounts for a fairly large chunk of the $67 billion lost to employee theft every year, many employers clearly don't agree.

RULE #4:
DO NOT WRITE ABOUT ANYTHING THAT COMPROMISES OR DISPARAGES YOUR COMPANY

Here's a better way to state this rule: "Don't write about or say anything you wouldn't want plastered on the front page of the New York Times next to your picture." This includes:

- Disclosing confidential information about your employer
- Hinting at or revealing your company's trade secrets
- Communicating proprietary information about your firm
- Bad-mouthing or naming co-workers disparagingly
- Criticizing your company's product or service
- Mentioning or disparaging the leadership of your firm
- Divulging anything negative about your job
- Including pictures of you at work

This also applies to HR-related information too. Every employer has valuable confidential information that it wants to keep under wraps. For example, it could be the HR strategy, the list of recruitment sources it uses, or its performance management process.

As an HR professional, violating this is morally and legally wrong. You have an obligation to preserve these secrets whether or not you signed a non-disclosure agreement. And, if you have signed an agreement and violate it, you could be liable for damages – and face a possible court order to cease and desist.

RULE #5:
IF YOUR BOSS OR COMPANY ABSOLUTELY WILL NOT SUPPORT YOUR INFOPRENEURING ENDEAVORS, THEN GO TO PLAN B.

In Plan B, you focus your infopreneuring activities on your hobbies, personal interests or on HR topics that are completely SEPARATE and APART from anything you do in your HR day job.

The idea here is to think about what you like to do away from work and then build a line of written reports around that topic. This could include things such as collecting antiques, gardening, golfing, biking, running, fixing up old cars, investing, cooking, real estate, interior design, arts & crafts, writing, speaking, weight loss, fitness, cancer survival/support, photography, pets, parenting, religion (e.g. Christianity) or travel.

Any activity that people do in their spare hours creates an opportunity for you to provide information that will help them enjoy it more, do it better, or make money at it. In taking this approach, there is no need to identify yourself by your HR day job as an employee of the "ABC Company" because it's not relevant. The only thing that matters is your know-how and expertise in that hobby or special interest.

Remember my story in Chapter 1. I started off in a non-HR niche (comic book collecting), before transitioning into my current HR niche. Follow this model. There are literally thousands of topics, markets and target audiences you can build your second income empire around. You can still follow the steps laid out in this book, just without all the HR examples. Let's say you're interested in gardening, but not sure what kind of report you could put together. Go to Amazon, search through all the books listed under "gardening" for ideas on what you might focus your own topic on…then give it your own unique twist and get it up and going using the rest of chapters in this book.

YOUR HR GOLDMINE

I'm not a lawyer and this is not legal advice, but there's nothing illegal, unethical or wrong with infopreneuring on the side as long as you:

- Do it on your own time, not at work.
- Don't use any of your company's resources (phone, computers, office supplies, phone, etc.)
- Don't compete with your company for business.
- Don't use, represent or make any references to your current company.
- Don't violate any company policies or employment

Why am I suggesting that you do this? Because, I want you to get started NOW and not wait. Experience is the best teacher. Even if you get started with a topic unrelated to HR. Just get going. You may ultimately transition into HR topics. After all, organizations change rapidly. Policies change. Bosses change too. You may change jobs. Waiting for the right time to get started or to go public with infopreneuring will delay your learning curve and the opportunity to build a second income.

Let me say this too...

I don't care how happy you are now in your HR role, if your company prohibits you from creating your own professional brand and identity away from work, you should do everything you can to find a new employer, because eventually you're going to feel very unhappy, underutilized and unfulfilled.

Today, any company that clamps down on its best talent and wants them to remain faceless and hide their personal expertise...and doesn't allow them to share this same expertise with the public...is holding that talent back from where the business world is going. You don't want to be left behind.

'Nuff said.

RULE #5:
BE READY TO SACRIFICE A LOT OF YOUR PERSONAL TIME

There are 168 hours in a week. If you subtract 56 hours for sleep (eight hours a day), you've got 112 left. If you give yourself another four hours a day for eating, travel, and taking care of personal needs, you've got 84 hours. Give yourself another 10 hours to have some kind of social life, and you still have 74 hours. Assuming you currently work 60 hours a week at your day job (nobody works 40 hours a week anymore in HR!), that means you've got 14 hours a week to be an infopreneur.

When you'll be able to use those free hours depends upon your schedule. If your HR gig is during the day, that pretty much limits you to evenings and weekends.

So, here are a few tricks and tips I've found helpful in utilizing this precious time:

Cut out TV. When I started infopreneuring, I watched less TV than ever before (eventually I watched none, though now I watch a few shows a week). For most HR folks, this one change will free up a couple hours a day or more.

Read less junk. I used to waste a lot of time reading and surfing the web just for entertainment. Same with magazines. I cut that stuff out early so I could focus on getting things done.

Go out less. I used to go to a lot of movies and out to dinner to socialize. I cut that out (mostly) for awhile, to make time.

Wake up earlier. Not everyone is going to do this but it was a good step for me. I found that I had more time to exercise and work on my reports in the morning before anyone woke up. The world was quiet and at peace and without interruptions

Leave work at a reasonable time. You know why you're too tired to do anything after work? It's because you stay there all night! Control how late you stay after work. If you come in at 7:00 am, plan your day so that you can end at a reasonable time and head home to work on your reports.

Exhaust all your vacation days. I had four weeks of vacation and I made sure to use all those babies up. I used one full week for a major vacation like a 5-day Caribbean cruise, then the rest of the time I used for my infopreneuring activities. I got out my calendar and scheduled things around holidays and weeks that I knew were clear for me to be out of the office. By doing it this way, I was able to put my full-time HR day job first and not piss off my boss for missing any important deadlines or events for the organization.

Maximize your lunch hour. If you must eat lunch at your desk, do double time while you're sitting there! Instead of surfing the web with one hand and holding a pickle in the other, use your break time to jot down ideas for potential reports. Personally, I carry a Levenger spiral notebook with me at all times – on the job, on my nightstand and in my briefcase, just in case I come up with a hot idea. I also jot down notes on the notes app on my iphone. All this really comes in handy when I have only a few snippets of free time during the day.

Set aside quiet time to be focused and organized. Just 30 minutes early in the day can fuel your mind and spirit with motivation. It can have a huge impact on the rest of the day. Rotate motivational or inspirational content around so it is fresh and has a more profound impact on you every day

Get your family involved. Whether it's proofreading or critiquing your work, giving family members the chance to help out is a great way to get more accomplished in less time -- while also making them feel like they're part of your new business.

These are the rules. If you follow them, you'll increase the chances of succeeding at infopreneuring without jeopardizing your HR day job.

14

ONE FINAL WORD: G.O.Y.A.

You've just been handed a detailed step-by-step roadmap that will enable you to turn your HR know-how into a second income empire and make a difference in people's lives. It tells you how you can start from scratch with a tiny, little 20-40 page written report and then grow this into a lucrative second income. And, oh yeah, you can accomplish all this without leaving your day job in HR.

There's only one thing left for you to do and it is to...

FOLLOW THE G.O.Y.A. METHOD:
Which Means Get Off Your Ass
...And Get Something Done!

Motion beats meditation. It's now time for you to get started. I can tell you what to do and how to do it, *but I can't make you do it.*

That's up to you.

You've got the blueprint and the playbook is right here within these pages. The step-by-step action plan is here too. And furthermore...YOU DON'T NEED TO DO EVERYTHING IN THIS BOOK. If you do just 20-30% of what's laid out here, you're well on your way to massive success.

YOUR HR GOLDMINE

At this point, the only person holding you back is YOU. The only one who is keeping you from making the commitment to get started is you. The only one making excuses for you is you! Trust me, you CAN be successful at this…if you will simply GET OFF YOUR ASS AND GET GOING TODAY!

What if you don't succeed the first time? That's easy. Just keep going. Every failure is a lesson. And what determines whether or not you will eventually succeed is what you learn from that lesson. So, my encouragement to you is to GET STARTED and STAY WITH IT!

If you do, believe me, there is going to come a time when you'll look back and say, "It was all worth it. If I hadn't been willing to do what was necessary back then, even when I wasn't sure what to do, I wouldn't be where I'm at today."

Winners don't quit. And if you've read this far, you're a winner!

So, let me close out by reminding you of a wise saying I learned years ago that has monumentally changed my life:

There are only two ways to get to the top of an oak tree.
One is to sit on an acorn and *wait*.
The other is to *start climbing*.

Start climbing and I'll see you at the top.

Onward!

Alan Collins

Alan Collins

CONNECT TO US ONLINE!
DISCOVER MORE WAYS TO SUCCEED IN HUMAN RESOUCES

Follow us on Twitter:
@SuccessInHR

Subscribe to our Blog:
SuccessInHR.com

"Like" us on Facebook:
Facebook.com/SuccessInHRDaily

Connect with us on LinkedIn:
http://LinkedIn.com/SuccessInHR

YOUR HR GOLDMINE

THE BRYAN A. COLLINS SCHOLARSHIP PROGRAM

The Bryan A. Collins Memorial Scholarship Program awards scholarship grants every year to minority students who demonstrate excellence in pursuit of their college degrees. Students selected for this scholarship must embody the values embraced by the late Bryan A. Collins -- great with people, great at academics and great in extra-curricular leadership activities.

Bryan Collins was a rising star and well-respected student leader at Tennessee State University. Bryan received his B.S. degree in Biology from TSU in May 2005. At the time of his passing, he was enrolled in the Masters program in physical therapy and anxiously looking forward to commencing his doctoral studies. On campus, he was a leader in the Kappa Alpha Psi fraternity, served on the Civic Committee, the Community Service Committee and help set strategic direction as a Board Member of the fraternity.

In addition, he found much success outside the classroom. He was voted Mr. Tennessee State first runner-up, was involved in the Student Union Board of Governors, was a founding member of the Generation of Educated Men and worked closely with the Tennessee State University dean of admissions and records.

Bryan found comfort and relaxation in sports, music, movies, video games, friends, good parties and just spending time with his family relaxing at home.

Key contributors to Bryan's scholarship program include the PepsiCo Foundation, the Motorola Foundation, Pamela Hewitt & Warren Lawson of Chicago and many other organizations and individuals. Additional details about Bryan, the scholarship program and how to contribute can be found at the scholarship website at: www.BryanCollinsScholarship.org.

YOUR HR GOLDMINE

ABOUT THE AUTHOR

Alan Collins is **Founder of Success in HR**, a company dedicated to empowering HR professionals and executives around the globe with insights and tools for enhancing their careers. He was formerly Vice President of Human Resources at PepsiCo where he led HR initiatives for their North American Quaker Oats, Gatorade and Tropicana businesses.

With 25 years as an HR executive and professional, Alan's corporate and operating human resources experience is extensive. He led an organization of 60 HR directors, managers and professionals spread across 21 different locations in North America, where he was accountable for their performance, careers and success. He and his team provided HR strategic and executional oversight for a workforce of over 7000 employees supporting $8 billion in sales. Alan also served as the HR M&A lead in integrating new acquisitions as well as divesting existing businesses; and he provided HR leadership for one of the largest change initiatives in the history of the Pepsi organization.

As the co-leader of the Quaker Tropicana Gatorade African American Network, Alan was selected as a member of the prestigious Executive Leadership Council, based in Washington D.C. He has also taught at various Chicago-area universities.

Alan is author of the *Unwritten HR Rules* and *Best Kept HR Secrets*. Both have been ranked among Amazon's top 10 books for HR professionals. In addition, he has written over 100 articles and special reports on HR that have appeared in *HR Executive Magazine, HRM Today* and other nationally-known publications for human resources professionals.

He received his BS and MS degrees in Industrial Relations from Purdue. More about Alan and his works can be accessed at: www.SuccessInHR.com.

Made in the USA
Lexington, KY
24 September 2012